Andrew D. Lester

SEX IS MORE THAN A WORD

BROADMAN PRESS
Nashville, Tennessee

Dewey Decimal Classification: 301.41
Printed in the United States of America

Photo Credits

Bob Combs
Steve Wall
Wallowitch
Steve Wall
Wallowitch
H. Armstrong Roberts
Rohn Engh
Wallowitch
H. Armstrong Roberts

CONTENTS

1. Sex Is More than a Word

You are presently involved in an important task, the search for identity. You are in the process of finding out "who you are becoming." This process is vital to your future happiness. It involves discovering and accepting who you are, learning what you expect of yourself, establishing your personal goals and objectives, deciding what you believe, and working out a life-style.

Sexuality is an important aspect of this process. Sex is a basic part of your identity, your personality, your selfhood. To become a whole person, a healthy mature person, you must have a healthy mature concept of yourself as a sexual being. If you do not accept that part of your identity and remain immature in your attitudes toward sex, then it will be difficult to become a fulfilled adult.

The decisions you make about how to express yourself sexually are among the most significant decisions you make during your teen-age years. These decisions establish the kind of sexual experiences and attitudes which you carry into adulthood and into marriage. You need as much information as possible about the physical, emotional, and psychological aspects of sexuality in order to make the best decisions. It is also important for you to develop a philosophy of life, a moral stance, a value system to use as criteria by which to make these decisions. The Christian faith provides principles and values which can be the backbone of your moral commitments.

The purposes of this book are (1) to provide information and knowledge which will help you accept sexuality as a positive, creative part of your personality, and (2) to help you develop healthy, mature, responsible ways of expressing and experiencing sexuality so that you can find fulfilment sexually, make mature decisions, prepare to be a happy sexual partner in marriage, and function as a responsible Christian individual.

It is very important for you to understand sex and sexuality. Many of society's ideas about sex and sexuality cause distrust between the sexes and hinder individuals in finding satisfying relationships with members of the opposite sex. Ideas which make males and females enemies, make exploitation and conquest the major motivations of male-female relationships, and imply that sexual behavior is degrading, are destructive to your goal of becoming a mature human being. The only way to see through these false generalizations is to inform yourself about sex and sexuality.

The Sexual Revolution

In the 1960's America went through a period of upheaval in its concept of sexuality. Many cultural changes contributed to this upheaval: (1) Development of sophisticated birth control devices (particularly the pill) reduced the possibilities of conception to a minimum allowing people to enjoy sexual intercourse with little fear of pregnancy. (2) Censorship has changed drastically, so that sexuality is frankly portrayed in words and pictures readily available to everyone. (3) Leisure time gives people more opportunity to involve themselves in situations which stimulate sexual interest and to participate in sexual activities. (4) Women are demanding freedom and equality with men in the area of sexuality and demanding change of the double standard. (5) Society is so mobile that fewer people have deep roots in their present community and are not as influenced by, and conforming to, traditional moral values, particularly in the area of sex.

This change in concepts about sexuality was called "the sexual revolution." Although many people (particularly churchmen) wailed and gnashed their teeth about this upheaval, the positive results should be noted. One important result was a decisive victory in the war against the Victorian view of sexuality which had controlled our culture (at least on the surface) for many years. The Victorian approach was one of suppression, but sex is no longer a taboo subject. It can be studied and talked about without fear of prosecution and reprisal. It is almost impossible for any group to defend an antisexual moral position and expect to be taken seriously.

The results of this "turn of the tide" are many. Sex and sexuality are accepted by most people as a good and natural part of human life. Sex is not as threatening as in the past. Women are now able to seek fulfilment and satisfaction in their sexual relationships. The rigid, legalistic rules about sexual behavior are broken down. Individuals have more freedom to decide, on the basis of their own value system and philosophy of life, how they want to express their sexuality. Sexual expression has been accepted as a valid experience of pleasure and excitement, whereas in the past it was the pleasure in sex that made it suspect.

Cultural Hang-ups

Despite the fact that "the sexual revolution" broke down old taboos, opened up new freedoms, and corrected many misconceptions and fears about sex, the society you live in is still in a quandary about how to handle sexuality. Our culture is preoccupied with sex, unsure about its meaning, and uncomfortable with its place in life.

CHANGE
EVERY
WED'
3 BIG UNIT
SEX SHOW
SHOES
LOVE
MATURE ADULTS ONLY
"BLONDE IN BLACK LACE"
ALSO EXTRA SHORTS
AND FEMMES FANTASTIQUE
ADULT ENTERTAINMENT
AT ITS BEST
8:30 AM to 2 AM.

The present situation can be described with words such as confusion, extremism, and experimentation. Every conceivable sexual behavior is practiced openly in our society. Sex saturates the mass media. The problem with this state of affairs is not the focus on sexuality, but the fact that many of the ideas and attitudes communicated by the mass media are misleading and degrading. The mass media often represent sex and sexuality in an unrealistic or unhumanistic light. There are precious few norms or standards not under attack by some group or other which believes differently.

Some aspects of "the sexual revolution" were negative. Some people, for example, took the idea of "sex is good and natural" (which it is) to the extreme of believing that since it is a natural physical desire, people should feel free to satisfy this physical need as easily as they drink when thirsty or eat when hungry. In our culture, however, sex is not only physical but it has significant psychological-emotional overtones. It is not like eating, urinating, and sleeping, because for humans, sex carries much more meaning than physical relief of biological tension.

Sex has lost its significance for many people. Much frustration and emptiness lie behind the frantic sexual preoccupation and activity in this society. Sexual freedom is established in our country, but sexual freedom is not in itself providing the way to a healthier development of masculinity and femininity. Sex can be among the most liberating and enriching of all human experiences. Sex can also be frustrating, disappointing, destructive, and tragic.

Americans have escaped Victorian bondage in their actions and in their conversations, but many have not escaped the emotional enslavement. Many Americans have not integrated a healthy view of sexuality into their personhoods. Counselors are still dealing with a high incidence of sexual maladjustments including fear, guilt, and anxiety. Sex is known scientifically, statistically, anatomically, and biologically, but the possible meanings and satisfactions of sexuality, its place in personal identity, are still missed by many individuals.

Our culture tends to identify sex with something physical, and the psychological and emotional meanings are not considered. For many people sex seems to be equated only with coitus or orgasm. If one experiences successful sexual intercourse, then he or she is thought to have reached sexual maturity. The ability to have sexual intercourse, however, is only a part of sexuality. Many feel that to master sexual stimulation techniques and learn the "how to" of lovemaking means they have attained sexual maturity. Virtually no competent author in the field of psychology and human behavior would defend this position. This is a symptom of our society. Concern over techniques and technology is uppermost while the concern with deep, profound human relationships becomes lost.

An Ethical Approach

Modern sciences, such as biology, physiology, sociology, and psychology, have discovered many truths about sexuality which enable the present-day Christian to understand much more about sex and sexuality than his forefathers. Science, however, does not provide a philosophy of sexuality or a value system to use in guiding sexual expressions. The disciplines of theology and ethics can offer an understanding of sexuality from this perspective. To rely on data from the sciences is important, but we have the responsibility to interpret this data in the light of our Christian faith. We believe that the true nature and meaning of human sexuality can be grasped only through an understanding of God's creation and his will for man.

Suggestions for Further Reading

Packard, Vance. *The Sexual Wilderness.* New York: David McKay Company, 1968.

Kirkendall, Lester A. and Robert N. Whitehurst. *The New Sexual Revolution.* New York: Donald W. Brown, Inc., 1971.

Hettlinger, Richard F. *Living With Sex: The Student's Dilemma.* New York: The Seabury Press. 1966.

Reuben, David. *Everything You Always Wanted to Know About Sex but Were Afraid to Ask.* New York: Bantam Books, 1969.

2. The Christian Faith and Sexuality

It is a sad fact that the Christian faith as proclaimed through the church has generally failed to help human beings understand and accept sex. Little positive guidance has been offered to young people as they struggle with their emerging sexuality. The stance of the Christian church through the centuries has usually been antisexual. The church has chosen two approaches to the subject of sexuality which have hindered its positive proclamation.

One approach has been to keep silent, ignore sex, and pretend that it was not a major concern for human beings of all ages. Well-meaning churchmen thought (and some still think) that it was immodest to talk about sex in church. The silence has communicated to many people, particularly young people, that sex is improper and "worldly." It implies that sex is of no interest to God, or perhaps is even disliked by him. It has been suggested that devoted Christians should not even think about sex much less experience it or discuss it!

Furthermore, the church has generally failed to talk about sex outside of marriage. It has been content to say, "Sex is all right in marriage," and let it go at that. The concerns of Christian young people about their growth and development as sexual persons is either ignored or spoken of so negatively that the young person feels guilty for thinking sexual thoughts and participating in sexual experiences.

The other approach taken by the church has been the "negative reaction" approach. In other words, when the church has spoken of sex, it has spoken against it (rather than for it) by speaking harshly, legalistically, and judgmentally. Sex has been described in its worst manifestations and attention called to all the ways in which sex can be misused. This approach resulted in the popular feeling that sex was evil and sexual sins the most repulsive of all.

As said above, the Christian stance toward sex has been negative, even antisexual, despite the attempts of a few men to the contrary. David Mace has pointed out three main reasons for these negative feelings.

One factor was the early church's disgust with the sexual behavior practiced in some parts of the world. As Christianity spread into the Greek and Roman worlds, its followers encountered societies which were extremely promiscuous. Social life included prostitution, extramarital relationships, homosexuality, and other questionable expressions of sexuality. Sex was divorced from love and seemed to be degrading and exploitative. The Christians of these earlier times responded negatively to this state of affairs and overreacted by thinking of sexuality as something bad and sinful.

A second factor was the prejudiced reading of the New Testament. The positive statements about sexuality mentioned by Jesus and Paul were overlooked and the negative ones emphasized. Jesus' comments on lust were taken to mean that all sexual desire and feeling was wrong. Paul's recommendation of celibacy (life without sexual relations with the opposite sex) was taken to mean that persons who refrained from sexual expression and experience were more pleasing to God than those who married and engaged in sexual intercourse. Paul also talked occasionally of marriage as if it were a concession to sexual drives and a necessary institution to guard against sexual evils—"it is better to marry than to be aflame with passion" (1 Cor. 7:9).

The third major factor contributing to the antisexual stance of the church, and probably the most important, was the influence of the philosophy called "dualism." This view of life was widespread in the Greek-Roman world of New Testament days. "Dualism" is the belief that man is composed of two separate things—a body and a soul (or flesh and spirit). It was believed that the body (flesh) was basically evil and the soul (spirit) was good. Therefore, the spiritual world was good and should be sought after by men. Since God was spirit, dualism believed that he did not like the flesh and considered it his enemy.

Sexuality, of course, is rooted in our physical existence and is expressed physically. Since the body and physical existence were considered bad, then sexual thoughts, feelings, and actions were considered displeasing to God. This dualism was taken into some of the early Christian theology and had a damaging influence on the church's concept of sexuality, for it soon decided that sex was basically evil and opposed to the true spiritual life.

Sex in Christian History

A brief description of the consequences of this negativism on the ideas and feelings toward sex in Christian history is in order. The great theologian, Augustine, who lived from A.D. 354 to 430, was responsible for many of the church's ideas on sexuality.

Augustine grew up in a Christian home and was cared for by a saintly mother. As he grew into adolescence and young adulthood, Augustine had trouble with his sexual growth and development. It is known from his autobiography that he had premarital sexual relations with at least two women, one of whom became pregnant by him. He tells about his tremendous struggle to control his sexual drives. Finally, at age 23, he was converted. His Christian experience seemed to center in his sexual struggle and was used by him to control, even to suppress, his sexual needs. Many young people still turn to religion as an excuse to suppress or deny sexual drives instead of using Christian truths to help them deal maturely with their sexual identity.

Because of his personal struggle, Augustine took a negative view of sex. He believed that sexual drives and needs were bad. He thought mankind was free from sexual drives until Adam and Eve sinned and that sexual drives were punishment for this sin. He further believed that through expressions of sexual desire original sin was passed between generations.

A second belief of Augustine's was that sex was wrong even in marriage unless the only motivation was the desire to produce children. He thought that it was better to remain single and have no sexual relations at all; if a person could not control his sexual drives, Augustine thought marriage was acceptable as a "remedy."

Augustine also passed on the belief that celibacy was the most sacred way of life. Since sexual desire was bad, he thought those who did not "give in to it" were better Christians than those who married and indulged. Since (as far as we know) John the Baptist, Jesus, and Paul chose to remain unmarried, he believed that abstinence from sexual relationships was a virture in God's sight. This idea is still present in the Roman Catholic insistence that the clergy must be celibate.

Later, other beliefs arose. The doctrine of the virgin birth was interpreted to mean that sexual intercourse was such an unclean business that Christ had to be conceived apart from human sexual functioning, and by a woman who never (as the Catholic Church believes it) engaged in intercourse.

These feelings about sexuality led to a distrust of woman. Since women stimulated male sexual feelings and desires, the male theologians placed on them the blame for orginal sin. The extremists felt that the devil worked through women to cause men's downfall into sexual sin. Women were not allowed to worship in some monasteries.

One would think that the Reformation would have changed some of these ideas, but that is not the case. Martin Luther and John Calvin did make marriage more important and valid in God's sight. Calvin, however, still thought celibacy was better than marriage and Luther still believed that sexual intercourse in marriage was a small sin, even though he said God would "wink at it."

Early American Culture

The church's negativism toward sexuality came to America embodied in the Victorian sex ethic. The same feelings toward sexuality became rooted in our culture. Sex was approached as basically an evil aspect of human existence. It was almost as if the devil, instead of God, had created sex. It was implied that God did not like sexuality and that the best Christians did not think or talk about it.

Sex in marriage was necessary (because of God's command to "multiply and fill the earth"), but it was not to be enjoyed. To find pleasure in sex was considered sinful. Sex was a taboo subject; it was not to be discussed at all. References to sex were considered improper and immoral. Jokes about sex were "dirty." Sexual expression outside of marriage was condemned. Masturbation and petting, among other things, were seen as shortcomings and very unchristian.

The double standard prevailed. Women were responsible for remaining virgins before marriage, and public censorship of unwed mothers was strong and harsh— such as the treatment given Hester Prynne in Hawthorne's work, *The Scarlet Letter.* It was thought that pious women were not to enjoy sex or want it. They were only to "do their duty" of satisfying their husbands and trying to become pregnant. Many women did not know they could experience orgasm.

Sex in the Church Today

It is easy to read the previous section and laugh at the history of narrow and fearful reactions to sex by the Christian church. However, many of these same attitudes are prevalent in most of today's churches. Many preachers and church leaders still think sex is "dirty" and an instrument of the devil. Churches are often afraid of anything sexual. Some Christians prohibit young people from dancing and swimming together for fear that sexual thoughts would occur. Sunday School classes are sexually segregated. Originally, this may have been to keep males and females from thinking about each other during the lesson.

Sex is still taboo in many areas. Ministers cannot use sexual words in the pulpit. Lessons on sexuality are not allowed, and church people fight sex education in the public schools. The extremists label those who support sex education or talk openly about it as Communists. Jokes which have sexual content are called "dirty." Dressing to accent one's masculinity or femininity is frowned upon. Exposure of the human body is considered socially improper and embarrassing.

It is sometimes indicated that to be "pure in heart" means a young person must rid himself or herself of any sexual thoughts or ideas and express no sexuality in their personality. An extreme example of this feeling is a lady who told me in a family life conference that "Jesus meets all my sexual needs." What a distortion of God's will for us as sexual beings! Certainly that is not Jesus' purpose in our lives.

In actuality not many Christians have any idea about what

Christianity has to say about sexuality. Most church members have no "theology of sex" through which to understand sexuality, build a sex ethic, or provide guidance about God's will for human sexuality. In fact, many churchmen still support ideas about sexuality which are not only foreign to the Christian faith, but actually unchristian.

The Bible and Sex

The Christian faith depends heavily on the Bible for its understanding of God, man, and the relationship between them. The biblical witness, as the Word of God, provides the cornerstone of wisdom and insight concerning God's divine purposes for creating humans as sexual beings and his will concerning sexual functioning. It must be admitted that this primary resource has been misused by many Christians in their attempts to deal with sex. It has been misused by both literalists and legalists for proof-texting while its primary messages went unnoticed.

Literalists interpret biblical passages in their word-for-word appearance, while neglecting the *context* in which they are found, overlooking their basic meaning, or without relating its message to the other messages of God's Word. An extreme example was Origen, a theologian in the third century, who took Matthew 19:12 literally and in his desire to live a higher spiritual life is said to have castrated himself (cut off his testicles). The possible errors of literalism are many. If the story of Rahab (Josh. 2 and Heb. 11:31) is taken literally, a case could be made for prostitution as a valid Christian vocation. If the story of Abraham and Sarah (Gen. 16:1-4) is taken literally, then every woman who could not bear children should arrange for her husband to have intercourse with someone else so he could father a child.

Legalists misuse the Bible by looking to it as a rule book with categorical answers to every sexual problem. In fact, the Bible gives no direct word on such things as birth control, abortion, or masturbation. The purpose of the Bible is to witness to the actions of God in history as a way of proclaiming his truths. Jesus did not come to bring more rules but to enable us to live more fully by recognizing the basic principles and truths of God's relationship to man and his wishes for man's existence.

At the other extreme are those who laugh at the Bible and discard it from consideration as a guide to understanding sex. They consider it an old book, written by fanatics with sexual hang-ups, who could not possibly have anything to say about sexuality in this day. Some blame the Bible for the negative view of sex which they hear from various churches and churchmen. They do not realize that sexual negativism is a misinterpretation of the Word of God.

The Bible does have authority for modern man. It presents ideas about the nature of man and the meaning of sexuality which have lasting truth. The Bible reveals basic principles of love and human relationships which give profound guidance for a creative and vital sex ethic. The next chapter shows how these principles are related to form the Christian interpretation of sexuality.

Suggestions for Further Reading

Mace, David R. *The Christian Response to the Sexual Revolution.* Nashville: Abingdon Press, 1970.

Blenkinsopp, Joseph. *Sexuality and the Christian Tradition.* Dayton, Ohio: Pflaum Press, 1969.

Cole, William Graham. *Sex and Love in the Bible.* New York: Association Press, 1959.

Feucht, Oscar E. et al. *Sex and the Church: A Sociological, Historical, and Theological Investigation of Sex Attitudes.* St. Louis: Concordia Publishing House, 1969.

Wynn, John C. (ed.). *Sex, Family and Society in Theological Focus: Some Divergent Views.* New York: Association Press, 1970.

White, Ernest. *Marriage in the Bible: Theological Guidance for Creative Pastoral Care.* Nashville: Broadman Press, 1965.

3. A Theology of Sexuality

The word "theology" refers to "the basic beliefs which the Christian faith holds about a subject." This chapter will discuss a theology of sex which is biblically based and grows out of the Christian understanding of God's work as Creator of the universe and his will for his human creatures.

In the Beginning

A theology of sexuality must start with the doctrine of creation. One way to understand yourself is to understand what God had in mind when he created man. The biblical account of creation states: "God said, Let us make man in our image, after our likeness. . . . So God created man in his own image, in the image of God created he him; male and female created he them" (Gen. 1:26-27).

God's Image. What does being created in God's image mean? Of course it doesn't mean that you look like him, since God is spirit. Actually it means that you are created with a spiritual personality. You are created in God's image in reference to your capacity to have fellowship with God, to be morally responsible to God, and to be free to choose how you will respond to the will of God.

Humans are part of the animal world, an integral part of the rest of creation and dependent on it. However, as a human you are distinctly different from the rest of creation because of your

God-image—because of your awareness of yourself, your freedom to choose, and your responsibility. You are also different in your ability to think, reason, and feel personal emotion. So you are a special part of the creation. God in his love has created you, given himself to you, and wills that you will respond to him and "love the Lord thy God with all thy heart, and with all thy soul, and with all thy mind, and with all thy strength" (Mark 12:30).

Being Human Is Good. Being human like God created you, then, is a good thing, not a bad thing as some would believe. It is important to remember that God called his creation "good." Many Christians talk about humanness as if it were a negative, as if God made a mistake in creating human beings. They feel as if an individual has two strikes against him or her just for being human. Those who feel this way dislike human emotions and feelings. They are suspicious of anger, sexuality, grief, and even intense joy and pleasure. Watch out for those (whether within the church or without) who degrade humanity and treat it as something basically bad that God is unhappy about. Your humanness is not a problem to God! He purposely created you this way!

Being Human Is Being Sexual. Being human includes many things, but the one of concern to us here is the fact that being human means you are sexual! This fact is so primary that it is the first aspect of our humanity mentioned by the Hebrew writer of Genesis—"male and female created he them." Yes, God purposely and positively created a bisexual (two sexes) world. He made men and women rather than one neuter creature.

Your sexuality is as basic to your personality as your potential for relating to God. In no way can an individual be described as human without including his or her sexuality. This is part of your "imageness," your spiritual personality. This means among other things that your sexuality is involved in your total style of life and that your total life is saturated with sexuality.

Any way you express yourself sexually is a reflection and a revelation of your whole personhood, your entire personality. Your sexual life is not only a biological, instinctual fact, but is an expression of your whole self.

Humanness Is Wholeness. The faith of the Hebrews passed down not only their perceptions of creation but also their perceptions of being human. They considered man to be a unified individual in whom the emotional, spiritual, mental, and physical aspects of existence are woven into one entity.

Sexual feelings and desires are basic and integral parts of God's creation of persons. This means that sexuality can never be seen as an evil part of man. Such a view is unbiblical. Sexuality should be accepted as not only a normal part of yourself, but as a gift and blessing from God.

It is a truth that whenever humanness, the nature of man, is degraded, sex will be degraded also. When human nature is understood as special and God's creation is treated with respect and dignity, then sex will be accepted as a creative fulfilling aspect of being human. Now consider the major meanings which sexuality has in God's purpose for you.

Sexuality and Personal Relationships

One of the basic purposes of sexual nature is to create an avenue by which humans can experience deep and profound personal relationships. It is the nature of personhood to need fellowship, love, and intimate contact with other persons. God's personhood, characterized by love ("God is love."— 1 John 4:8), is needful of personal relating. The Christian faith has always believed God himself wants fellowship. One purpose of the Christian doctrine of the Trinity is to express the fellowship within God. The Christian doctrine of creation has believed that one facet of God's purpose in creation was to have creatures with whom to relate.

Part of your "God's image" is to find fulfilment in meaningful relationships with others. Love, by its very nature, seeks out others to whom it can give and from whom it can receive. The gift of sexuality has provided man with the most complete way of expressing and sharing the love God has made possible for him to experience. Without these loving relationships, man is alone and isolated.

Humans Need the Other Sex. The author of Genesis conveys an important truth when he writes, "Then the Lord God said, It is not good that the man should be alone; I will make a helper fit for him' " (2:18 RSV). Humans by themselves are lonely. When not involved with others they are isolated. The creation story in Genesis 2 (which details the creation of women) points out the incompleteness of man's nature without women (the other sex). When God recognized man's loneliness, he had all the birds and animals brought before the man, but none was adequate—"but for the man there was not found a helper fit for him" (2:20 RSV).

But God had yet another plan. He created woman— and man immediately recognized woman to be his completion, his fulfilment. She appeared the same, but was radically different. "Then the man said, 'This at last is bone of my bones and flesh of my flesh: she shall be called Woman, because she was taken out of Man' " (2:23 RSV). The Hebrew writer sums up his understanding of the significance of this mutual fulfilment and completion by saying, "Therefore a man leaves his father and his mother and cleaves to his wife, and they become one flesh" (2:24 RSV).

"One Flesh." With this statement the writer symbolically explains the sexual drive and the complementarity of the sexes. Man and woman were originally one flesh, and it is their destiny to become one flesh again. What does becoming one flesh mean? Of course the most obvious meaning includes all

that is said above about the relationship between sexual intercourse and the need for biological oneness, but the concept includes much more. In the physical sex act two individuals express a union and completeness of two selves, two unique personalities, rather than just two bodies.

The two separate, independent persons (male and female) choose to create a special relationship in which their personhoods complement and fulfil one another. This new relationship does not obliterate their individual personalities, but it does bring into existence a new aspect of living for both parties and creates something new. One of the most significant ways in which the depth of their need, the meaning of their love, and the intimacy of their relationship is expressed is through sexual experience.

"To Know." A second description of the way in which sexual relationships build communion in man-woman relations is through the concept of "to know." The first reference to sexual intercourse in the Bible uses the verb "to know" as a synonym for sexual intercourse—"Now Adam *knew* Eve his wife, and she conceived and bore Cain" (Gen. 4:1). Matthew uses the same phrase to refer to sexual intercourse when discussing the marriage of Joseph and Mary—"he took his wife, but *knew* her not until she had borne a son" (Matt. 1:24-25 RSV).

Why would the biblical writers use such a term to signify sexual intercourse? Rather than merely being delicate, they were describing a profound meaning of sexual intercourse. The word in Hebrew means "being acquainted with," "to know well," "to experience"; so it is more than intellectual knowing. It is a "knowing" from experiencing.

Sexual intercourse provides "knowledge" of a human of the opposite sex. We "know" what we lack, as either a male or a female, by experiencing it in intimate, revealing relationships with one of the opposite sex. This intimate "knowing" reaches its most profound level in intercourse. A human being, whether male or female, knows himself and his own potential through experiencing the powerful fulfilment of intercourse. This person also comes to know his partner in a way that cannot be achieved through any other avenue of experience.

Sexuality by itself cannot provide this profound type of relationship. Love, in all of its manifestations and commitment, must be present before "knowing" becomes meaningful. A true, loving, one-flesh relationship has a level of profound "knowledge" which is deeper than other relationships.

God created humans incomplete without the opposite sex and provided a way for fulfilment through sexuality. This is another expression of man's loneliness and the power of sex to bring relationships into his life. Man was not attracted sexually to the animal world and could not find deep satisfaction with these creatures. It was only through union with woman that man found satisfaction and oneness.

A Christian view of sex and sexuality must include the realization that sexual intercourse, which provides a sense of completion and unity through biological desire, is an important value. Furthermore, though the fulfilment of this sexual drive for union may result in conception, the basic value of sexual intercourse is not related to the desire or expectation of having children. The Christian must accept the fact that a real aspect of the dignity of sex is its function in providing union and completeness through physical means (drives and needs) which are both emotional (psychological) and biological.

Sexuality and Procreation

A second purpose which God had for creating a bisexual world and providing humans with sexual desires and drives was to involve them in the continuing process of creation. "Procreation" means to create with or for and makes reference

to the fact that through sexual intercourse women conceive and bear children. Within a woman the male sperm joins the female egg and a potential human life begins. This event is sacred in the sense that humans are using a gift of God (sexuality) to join him in the creation of a new life. This is a significant responsibility under God and should never be taken casually. Conceiving and bearing children can be a very meaningful experience to a man and woman who love one another and seek to share this love through parenting.

Marriage Is the Context

The most obvious result or consequence of God's purposes for creating you as a sexual being (personal relationships and procreation) is the establishment of a marriage relationship. The author of Genesis says that because of the meaning which sex can have in fulfilling humans of both sexes, "a man leaves his father and his mother and cleaves to his wife, and they become one flesh" (2:24 RSV). So marriage becomes the relationship in which two individuals (of different sexes) meet each other's need for sexual expression and for "knowing" another human in a profoundly different way than in other relationships. Within the one-flesh relationship, a man and a woman overcome their isolation and loneliness by knowing each other through sexual expression and may choose to join with God in the creative process through procreation.

Suggestions for Further Reading

Bailey, D. S. *The Mystery of Love and Marriage.* London: SCM Press, Ltd., 1952.

White, Ernest. *Marriage and the Bible.* Nashville: Broadman Press, 1965.

Howell, John C. *Teaching About Sex: A Christian Approach.* Nashville: Broadman Press, 1966.

Bertocci, Peter A. *Sex, Love, and the Person.* New York: Sheed & Ward 1967.

Grimm, Robert. *Love and Sexuality.* Trans. David Mace. New York: Association Press, 1964.

4. Sexual Development and Sexual Expression

Puberty

Puberty refers to the period in life when your body changes into a fully matured, sexually capable body. At this point you become physically capable of reproduction. Slowly the first signs of puberty appear. You begin to grow and fill out. Hair begins to grow in places it did not appear before, first in the genital region where your sex organs are located and then under your arms. The boy also experiences hair growth on his face and other parts of his body. For some this hair growth is light; for others it is heavy and thick, depending on heredity. Neither the amount of hair nor its thickness has anything to do with sexual maturity.

Physical figures are changing also. The boy's shoulders begin to broaden and he slims down at the hips. The girl is widening at the hips and her body becomes rounded and soft (and she hopes, curvaceous). The boy's voice begins to change, either gradually or more rapidly and marked with occasional "breaks." The perspiration glands mature rapidly at puberty and cause problems with your complexion (particularly on the face) as well as body odor.

The age at which puberty occurs varies greatly. It is easier to establish when the girl reaches puberty because of her menstrual cycle. About 75 percent of the girls in our culture have their first menstrual cycle between the ages of twelve and fifteen. Of the other 25 percent about half will have their first menstrual period before twelve years of age and the other half after fifteen years of age.

Boys do not have one particular physical development around which puberty is centered. It takes about two years from the start of puberty until it is completed. The *average* age at which puberty begins in boys is around thirteen.

As you can see, females generally reach puberty about two years earlier than boys and are naturally interested in heterosexual relationships at an earlier age. This explains why some girls find many of the boys in the seventh, eighth, and ninth grade classes to be childish and immature, like younger brothers. It also explains why some boys feel so uncomfortable with the girls in these same grades. It is not until high school that males, as a group, "catch up" in their sexual development.

Male Sexual Experience

Many new happenings, both physical and emotional, are part of the male's experience during puberty. Unexpected erections is one of the first physiological events to occur. They may come at anytime, under almost any circumstances. Sometimes it is embarrassing, and the boy wonders whether or not others around him, particularly females, are noticing this physical happenstance. The penis seems to operate on its own wave length and the male can rarely control these spontaneous erections. They may occur in times of stress, in times of fright, and even when angry. They may occur during the excitement of a sporting event or simply because of friction created by clothing on the genital area.

Most stimulation, of course, is sexual and comes from thoughts and fantasies about females or during actual heterosexual contacts. Most males seek out this stimulation during their adolescent years from movies, books, and the sexual pictures in magazines which they manage to obtain and keep for frequent referral. Many males in adolescent years keep stacks of nude pin-up cards or suggestive magazines and books hidden in their rooms. This kind of curiosity about experiences with sex is not abnormal.

Nocturnal emissions ("wet dreams") are another normal occurrence during adolescence. They are caused by the build-up of sperm in the testicles which must be released to keep the body chemically balanced. It is a physiological happening, usually occurring at night. It is not unusual for these ejaculations to be accompanied by romantic sexual dreams. Sometimes you are not even aware of the emission until finding stiff stains on your pajamas or bedsheet the next morning. At other times you remember awakening just before or during the ejaculation and feeling the warm release of semen and the following relaxation of your body. The sperm which your sexual glands are now producing is in the semen (the milky fluid expelled from the penis). You are now physiologically able to impregnate a girl.

Ejaculations are also brought about by consciously choosing to stimulate the genitals with your hands or some object. Stimulating one's self in this manner is called masturbation. The usual result is orgasm, the very pleasurable experience which seems something like "the bursting of a pipe." There is a physical rush ending in a strong muscular movement and contractions throughout the body but particularly in the pelvic region. The body usually feels warm and relaxed after this experience.

In times past many young people were taught by their parents and other adults that masturbation was a horribly evil act which no Christian young man would practice. Young men were sometimes told that they would become sterile, impotent, mentally ill, or homosexual if they "played with themselves." You probably know now that scientific investigation reveals no negative physical results from masturbation. It does not harm the body, the mind, the nervous system, or the sexual organs.

One reason given by those who considered masturbation a sin is the story of Onan recorded in Genesis 38. This story has been used as a proof text concerning the evils of masturbation. If you will read the story carefully, you find that Onan was not masturbating, but was having sexual intercouse with Tamar, his dead brother's wife. His act was not masturbation, but "coitus interruptus" (which means withdrawing the penis from the vagina after lovemaking but before ejaculation). However, God's dissatisfaction with Onan was not because of spilling his seed on the ground, but because by doing this Onan failed to be loyal to the Jewish custom called levirate marriage. This custom and law said if a man died without having a son to continue his name, then a brother or other male kin should impregnate his widow until she conceived a son. Neither this story nor any other in the Bible actually mentions or condemns masturbation.

From a Christian ethic, masturbation is in itself neither good nor bad, but simply an experience of sexual growth and development. Masturbation takes on positive or negative value depending on its meaning and purpose in a male's life. During early adolescence masturbation is normally a way of relieving sexual tension (with which God created us). It also serves as an expression of growing masculine desire for sexual intimacy with a female and as a way of experiencing one's developing sexual potential. This can be a healthy experience. If guilt and fear become part of it, however, it can become unhealthy and leave emotional scars.

Like almost any other aspect of our lives, masturbation can become a problem. It is possible that you could get so carried away with the pleasures of physical relief and emotional excitement through fantasizing or daydreaming about sexual scenes that masturbation becomes your main sexual expression. Substitution of masturbation for the normal heterosexual interaction of a high school student is a symptom of possible emotional problems.

Sexual love, by its very nature, reaches out to people of the opposite sex and desires to relate profoundly to them at all levels: emotional, mental, spiritual, and physical. In high school years masturbation should become secondary to this interest. Some boys will use masturbation for sexual relief throughout adolescence even though it normally loses some of its meaning at this point in life. In fact, you may find it more of a necessity, something you can't resist doing, rather than something you plan for.

Nighttime dreams (unplanned) and fantasies (things you imagine in you mind) which occur while you are awake, may create mixed feelings. It is rewarding to dream about and imagine sexual conquests, but they may seem indecent or immoral to you and produce some anxiety and guilt. Most of the dreams are grandiose and represent the male's wish to become a strong, desirable, masculine individual. Sometimes these dreams revolve around several sexually appealing (almost always unknown) women who are greatly impressed with you, openly display their sexuality, and take initiative in lovemaking. Other dreams may include a desirable woman who is at first resistive to your charm but changes her mind because of something you are able to do, such as saving her life, winning a big game, or some other heroic deed. Later in teen-age years the dreams and fantasies begin to focus on one girl at a time. The girl may be identifiable as someone you know in real life, such as your girlfriend or other girls with whom you are sexually impressed.

Female Sexual Experience

Girls experience puberty in a more dramatic way because of menstruation and breast development. The first menstrual cycle is a unique experience for the female. Her body has signaled that it is becoming sexually mature. What happens during menstruation? One of the egg cells contained in your ovaries ripens. The rest of your body prepares for the conception of a child. The lining of the uterus thickens with blood and tissue to provide a place for the fertilized egg to grow. When the egg leaves the ovary and is not fertilized by a male sperm, then nature "empties the room" your body prepared for a guest that did not arrive.

Menstruation reminds you every four weeks that you are a woman, not a little girl. You now have the capacity to undertake the female privilege of conception, pregnancy, and birth. This physical happening often enables the girl to accept her "womanness" more quickly than the boy can accept his manness."

How do you react to your menstrual cycles? The responses differ greatly from girl to girl. Some girls have no physical side effects from menstruation. Others have mild cramps or abdominal pain. About 50 percent have side effects which are bothersome enough to consult a physician.

More important is how you respond emotionally to your menstrual cycle. Your attitude will be affected by different things such as (1) your mother's feelings toward menstruation which she may have passed on to you, (2) your feelings toward your own body, and (3) your feelings about being a female.

Your mother may have been raised in a home where menstruation was considered a necessary evil, something a woman had no choice but to accept and live with. She may have passed this attitude on to you without your even realizing it. If your mother was disgusted with this aspect of womanhood, then you might be also. If she accepted menstruation as part of womanhood and was proud of her "womanness," then you probably are also. You may choose to bear children in the future or you may not, but the capacity to bear children is a primary factor making you a woman and, hopefully, can be accepted by you as a valid sign of "womanness."

What do you think of your body? If you feel that your physical body is not good, if you feel that bodily functions, like urination and bowel movements, are dirty, if you don't like the way you look or the shape of your body, then you probably don't think positively about menstruation. If you think your body is okay, feel comfortable about bodily functions, and like the way you look, then you have probably accepted menstruation as a potentially good part of life.

How do you feel about being a woman? If you wish you had been a boy, if your parents look down on women, if you are afraid of womanly endeavors like pregnancy and childbirth, or if you don't like what is expected traditionally of women in our society, then you probably resent menstruation as a sign of enslavement. If the opposite of these things is true, you probably think of menstruation in a positive way, not that you enjoy it, but that you accept it as a sign of womanhood.

Various studies have demonstrated that the amount of physical pain and discomfort a woman experiences, and the extent to which depression and other moods bother her, often depends on her attitudes toward menstruation. Those who have the positive feelings and accept menstruation have less physical pain and discomfort and fewer "bad" moods than do women who have negative feelings about their femininity.

The other major sexual development for a girl is the growth of her breasts. The development of your breasts probably began before menstruation and in fact, gave you some idea of what was to come. The breasts begin to bud early in puberty and usually mature within three years. In mature young women there is a considerable difference in breast size. Some have small breasts, some medium, and some large. Shapes are also different. Some are rounded, some are more flat, and some shaped like a cone.

Just as the boy worries about the size of his penis, so you may worry about the size of your breasts. If you have small breasts, you may wonder whether or not you are as much of a woman as your friends with medium and large breasts. You must remember that sexual attractiveness is not necessarily related to size and shape but to how a woman feels about herself and how she can project that feeling. What you think about your physical endowments and how you feel about your "womanness" is more important to males than your physical measurements. Your breasts will be attractive to those boys who like you and special to the one who loves you.

Masturbation is something most girls in the past did not experience. Since your sexual feelings are not focused on your genitals, your sexual satisfaction at puberty and afterward will often come from other things than actual physical manipulation of the genitals. However, as you have matured you are much more aware of your sexual potential than previous generations. Because of the knowledge you have about the female's abilities to experience sexual pleasure and orgasm, because of the romantic-sexual stimulation you receive from literature and movies, and because of the lovemaking which you may engage in while dating, you may have experimented with masturbation and many will engage in it regularly. Neither the physical satisfaction of masturbation nor the emotional fantasies which accompany it are abnormal.

Lovemaking

Now that we have described some aspects of your individual sexual development, let us talk about what happens when your sexuality comes into contact with the sexuality of a person of the opposite sex. The word "lovemaking" here refers to the normal, expected, sexual communication and experience shared in our time by people in love.

Each of you must decide at every moment within the loving relationships you establish with boyfriends or girlfriends what levels of lovemaking are appropriate, responsible, ethical possibilities for you and your date, steady, or fiancee.

We can talk about lovemaking more creatively by describing the development of sexual expression within a loving relationship between two actual teen-agers. We will use the story of two young people who came to me for counseling because of their concern about the sexual aspects of their relationship. They were high school seniors, fairly mature, basically honest and responsible. We will call them Ron and Kate.

Ron and Kate had been dating for seven months. They liked each other very much. They had several previous dating relationships in which they had learned a lot about themselves and the opposite sex. Neither of them needed to "prove" their sexuality and they had allowed their relationship to develop at a casual pace. They enjoyed each other's company, they have similar interests, and Ron's sense of humor makes them laugh a lot. Kate was proud to be seen with Ron and felt grateful that he liked her. The following is a brief description of the development of their sexual relationship which they discussed in detail.

Ron and Kate enjoyed holding hands, kissing, and embracing. Not long after they began dating steadily, they found "soul-kissing" (French-kissing, deep kissing, etc.) to be a type

of lovemaking they enjoyed. Their expression of sexuality intensified one night when Ron had spontaneously put his hand over Kate's breast. The experience was exciting for both of them. Kate had been somewhat hesitant at first but had relaxed and enjoyed the feeling. Later that night Ron had put his hand up under her blouse and touched her bare skin. Kate had pulled away and asked Ron to stop, which he did. Ron apologized to Kate but she told him not to worry.

I asked what happened to each of them after they got home that evening. Ron had been quite excited and fantasized about sexual intercourse. The excitement and tension led to masturbation. He had also worried about what Kate might think about him since he already liked her a great deal. Kate said she had enjoyed being touched and liked feeling the excitement which this had created in Ron. She was confused by the hesitant feeling she had that something was wrong. She could not understand why an experience which she considered pleasurable and loving could cause her any concern.

Several nights later Ron touched her breast again "to see if it would be okay," he said. She had squeezed his neck to let him know it was okay and fondling of her breasts became a regular part of their lovemaking. Ron said this meant a great deal to him and was a way of expressing his affection and care for Kate. She was enjoying this more than she ever imagined. Their relationship was so open that they could talk about their lovemaking, and even decided at this point to try to limit intensive lovemaking to a certain number of nights per month.

The next major event in their expression of sexuality was during an evening of intense lovemaking when Ron suddenly had an orgasm. He indicated that it had been very embarrassing and he wondered what Kate was thinking. He worried that she would be repulsed or frightened. Kate said that she had not realized what happened at first, but when she did she was a little shaken. Her feelings were confusing again. She was glad that Ron could have such an intense physical response to their lovemaking, yet she was uneasy about the strength of these emotions.

They did not feel as free to talk about this part of their sexual expression as about the fondling, but it often occurred as the climax to an evening of lovemaking. When I asked about the results, they mentioned two positives and two negatives. The positives were: (1) Ron said he did not go home as tense and frustrated sexually and did not need to masturbate "to put himself to sleep," and (2) Kate felt less concerned about Ron's sexual needs and "setting limits" since his sexual drives diminished immediately after this experience.

They both realized that this diminishing of sexual energy caused one of the negative results. Sometimes after Ron had an orgasm, the togetherness and closeness felt by each of them would wear off and a feeling of "emptiness and distance" would arise. On these occasions their relationship did not seem as wonderful after orgasm as it had during the hours before. The second negative was expressed by Kate. When Ron would reach a climax she was usually left very stimulated and frustrated ("high and dry," as she called it).

Ron's realization of this fact led to the event several weeks earlier which brought them to a counselor. On that evening they ended up alone at Kate's house. She was unusually happy and both sensed her strong sexual needs. Ron eventually ended up caressing her until she came to climax.

Ron and Kate had entered into a difficult area of life and love. To continue making love at this level would make sexual intercourse a natural and easy next step, but that step involves many more difficulties than can be imagined in the heat of a lovemaking situation.

They realized their situation demanded serious consideration. They felt themselves to be in love, cared for one another, and did not want their relationship to be disrupted or sabotaged. The intensity of their sexual experience was meaningful to them. However, their positive feelings were mixed with some doubts and uncertainties. They sensed the possibility that their sexual experience could outdistance their developing personal relationship and effect it in a negative manner. It was at this point they decided to see a counselor.

The next three chapters describe the subject matter that Ron, Kate, and myself talked about during our sessions. You may have had experiences similar to Ron and Kate's, or you may not have had this much sexual experience, or you may have gone beyond. Whatever the extent of your experience, the following chapters will help you evaluate your own feelings, thoughts, and beliefs about sexuality and help you make decisions about the expression of sexuality.

Suggestions for Further Reading

Barnett, Len. *Sex and Teen-agers in Love*. Surrey, England: Denholm House Press, 1967.

Glassberg, Bert Y. *Teen-age Sex Counselor*. Barron's Educational Series 1965.

Rubin, Isadore, and Lester A. Kirkendall. *Sex in the Adolescent Years*. New York: Association Press, 1968.

Shedd, Charlie W. *The Stork Is Dead*. Waco, Texas: Word Books, 1968.

Jersild, Arthur T. *The Psychology of Adolescence*. New York: The Macmillan Co., 1963. See chapter on sexual development.

Horrocks, John E. *The Psychology of Adolescence*. Boston: Houghton Mifflin Co., 1962. See chapter on sexual development.

5. Christian Values and Sexual Expression

Ron and Kate were both committed to God and the Christian faith. They had begun to wonder how their faith could help them understand the meaning of their relationship and evaluate future possibilities from a Christian perspective. The increasing sexual expression in their relationship had not developed with any careful thought about Christian ethics. Now they were interested in learning about a Christian theology of sexuality and understanding how Christian ethical principles could be applied to heterosexual relationships and particularly to the expression of sexual feelings. Ron and Kate found the following principles helpful in evaluating the development of their sexual relationship.

It is much easier to give rules and regulations rather than principles (perhaps that is why many adults and churches do it), but this would be unfair and unbiblical. Your freedom and responsibility under God for making choices in your life about your own sexuality must be taken seriously. These principles are applicable to every expression of sex from holding hands to sexual intercourse. They apply to expressions of sexuality both before and after marriage. Of course, the chapter on theology underlies this discussion.

Sex and the Whole Person

The creation story teaches that God created us as sexual

beings and that sexuality is an integral part of human personality. Sex cannot be separated from the rest of personal existence. Ethically speaking, expressions of sexuality should be expressions of total personality.

Most expressions of sexuality are rooted in the biological aspects of personhood, fueled by sexual drives. This is as it should be. Ethically, however, sexual expression should be much more. It should also represent the psychological self, meet emotional needs, and be related to one's philosophy of life and value system. Expressions of sexuality which are related only to the physiological aspects of personality fall short of their potential.

This principle also means that the total personality of a sexual partner must be taken seriously. When only the physical sexual aspects of a partner are considered, then his or her psychological self, emotional needs, and philosophy of life are not cared for and the principle of wholeness is violated.

Sex and Personal Relationships

One of God's purposes in creating us as sexual persons was to provide an avenue by which to express and experience personal relationships. An ethical translation of this belief would suggest that expressions of sexuality should take place in the context of established personal relationships. Sexual activity which is impersonal, or outside of a personal relationship, falls short of the Christian ideal.

The relationship between a prostitute and a client, for example, is usually a physical relationship rather than a personal one. Neither partner is ordinarily known to the other. The contract (reason for getting together) has nothing to do with understanding, loving, or knowing each other. The contract is for an exchange of sexual experience in which biological relief is sold by one and bought by the other. The sexual act is not an expression of total personality, but one in which the physical aspect of personhood is basically the only one expressed. A casual pickup date in which sex is the only objective is the same. Expressions of sexuality which are only biologically motivated fall short of the potential meanings which exist in human sexuality.

Sex Is Good

The Christian faith believes that sex is good and that God purposely created us as sexual beings! Our sexual nature provides one avenue of experiencing personal fulfilment and abundant life. What meaning does this belief have for Christian ethics? Sexual expression is good when it brings meaning and fulfilment to an individual's life. When sex is serving this purpose of furthering God's will for people to become fully mature human beings, then that sexual expression is good. When a sexual experience is detracting from an individual's life, emptying instead of fulfilling, pulling down instead of lifting up, destructive rather than creative, then that expression of sexuality is negative and contrary to God's purposes.

Sex and Communication

Another purpose involved in our creation as sexual beings is that our sexual nature is a vehicle for communication between the sexes. Communication here does not mean something simple such as a broadcast or a poster. It refers to a way of revealing one's self to another person whom we want to know us completely. Communication in the broadest sense means "to connect," "to impart," "to convey," and "to make known." To really communicate means to make oneself understood, to share one's deepest thoughts and feelings.

A word which comes from the same root is the word "communion," which describes the Lord's Supper. Communion means "to participate in and mutually share," usually referring to a special event or a particular relationship.

Marriage should be a "communion relationship," one in which the partners participate in and share intimately the life of each other. One avenue through which such communion takes place is through sexual relationships.

The biblical use of the verb "to know" as a synonym for sexual intercourse refers to the role of sexual relationships in helping individuals understand and know themselves and their sex partners. Sexual behavior always communicates something. The Christian ethic is concerned about whether or not the communication is of something personal, profound, honest, and within the context of love. When communication is at this level, then sexual expression is valid; but when sexual expression is not an attempt at sharing and revealing one's self, then it is suspect. When young people are relating to someone they do not feel comfortable with, do not trust, do not want to share their thoughts and feelings with, or to whom they are afraid to reveal themselves, then intimate sexual expression will not be an expression of communion.

Sex and Integrity

In dating relationships sexual expression should be *honest* communication of the feelings which each person has toward the other. Each partner has the responsibility of communication through sexual activity only that which he or she really feels. An individual who expresses sexually more intimacy than he or she really feels toward the other person is guilty of miscommunication. The other person in such a situation does not have an honest evaluation of the partner's feelings. He or she responds, therefore, to something that is false. One negative result of this false communication is that one partner becomes more involved than the other and gets hurt.

When a man says, "I love you," to his girl friend only because he knows this will "open her up" for sexual intimacies, then he is dishonest and misleading in his sexual approach. Both males and females in our society are taught to use elaborate and deceitful tactics in order to manipulate and take sexual advantage of each other. They use both physiological and emotional methods of "setting up the other." Our society seems to teach males that sexual conquest is a valid and manly act. From the Christian perspective, however, sexual conquest is an unethical way of relating to another person, regardless of whether the male or the female takes the initiative.

Many young people are learning to be more honest in their expression of sexual need and talking more about their sexual feelings and how these feelings can be expressed. A loving expression of sexuality would not use another individual for personal gain. Reuel Howe has pointed out that God made *things to be used* and *people to be loved,* but many individuals operate in reverse, that is they *love things* and *use people.*

Christians recognize and accept the personal integrity of every other human. They respect their rights, their interests, and their freedom. Other individuals are not used as a means to an end. Much in American culture suggests that the opposite sex is to be used. It is implied that females should use their charm to trap the right man, to gain security, or to achieve status. Males are taught to use the female as a conquest or a prize in order to build up his sense of manliness without any thought to her needs or personhood. This is unethical and contradictory to the basic principle of love.

Mutual Meaningfulness in Sex

The subject of using and manipulating people brings another principle into focus which can be called "mutual meaningfulness." This principle believes that sexual expression between two people should have the same meaning to each partner. Both should be emotionally invested in the sexual interaction

and equally involved in giving and receiving these sexual expressions. If either partner is demanding sexual favors without the other's involvement, then this sexual interchange is not based on an ethic of love. When one partner demands sexual favors from the other partner without concern for his or her feelings, needs, and desires, then the sexual relationship is not mutually meaningful and falls short of the principle of love.

Sex and Responsibility

A Christian ethic concerning sexuality must consider the principle of responsibility. A Christian sex ethic is measured not only by what one does but also by how much responsibility one takes for the sexual expressions in which he or she participates. A person's sexual maturity can be evaluated by how he or she perceives and accepts results of sexual experiences. The obvious concerns which should exist between two young people who are considering sexual intercourse is an example. What are the possible consequences for which they must be willing to take responsibility?

Physically speaking there are the obvious possibilities of pregnancy and venereal disease. What if one partner is discovered later to have a venereal disease, will he or she take responsibility to communicate that to the other, and will both take responsibility for getting medical help? Or will they pretend it is unimportant and risk infecting others?

Will the couple take responsibility in advance for using some birth control device to protect against unwanted conception, or will they run the risk of pregnancy? Or suppose they participate in sexual intercourse, and conception does occur. Will they take serious responsibility for dealing with the conceptus (the beginning stage of life in the womb)? Will they weigh the alternatives of abortion, adoption, keeping the child, and getting married—trying to make the best decision for all concerned? Or will they make some hurried, panicky decision that multiplies the problem? Will each partner accept a share of the responsibility or will each blame the other and "pass the buck?" Will the father stand faithfully by the mother as she carries out the options, or will he leave her alone to carry this burden?

Emotionally there are other concerns which the partners should share. How will they handle the emotional consequences such as guilt, hurt, regrets, fears, and loss of self-esteem? Will each partner be willing to commit himself or herself to bringing about healing and reconciliation if this sexual behavior has negative results? Or will they take the attitude of "Sorry, baby, that's your problem." These same questions (about accepting emotional-psychological consequences) should be asked about any type or level of lovemaking.

A Christian must be willing to take responsibility for the consequences of his sexual behavior. This includes responsibility for its effect on him or her personally as well as a willingness to stand by and participate in the consequences to the partner. Willingness to share the consequences with the partner is a demonstration of the "faithfulness" of love. The individual who cannot be faithful in the aftermath of sexual behavior and who is unwilling to struggle with the consequences is immature and either unable or unwilling to operate within the context of *love*.

Sex and Love

The principle of love should undergird every aspect of sexual expression. When asked to describe which commandment was the greatest (or in other words, what is the most important principle we should follow), Jesus answered, " 'The Lord our God, the Lord is one; and you shall love the Lord your God with all your heart, and with all your soul, and with all your mind, and with all your strength.' The second is this, 'You shall love your neighbor as yourself. There is no greater commandment than these.' " (Mark 12:29-31 RSV). All the principles we are discussing are related to loving in the New Testament sense.

In almost every discussion of sex, love, and marriage with a group of young people someone raises the twin questions, "How do you know if you are in love?" and "How do you know that someone is really in love with you?" One of the most difficult things for young people to decide is the difference between real love and impostors (such as infatuation and sexual attraction). What is love? Here are some of its basic characteristics.

1. Love is interested in the *whole person* while impostors are interested only in one aspect of the loved person, for example, her beauty or his money. A maturing love cares for every aspect, every part of the beloved's life. A young person in love is interested in the other person's school work, vocational plans, the rest of the family, and all the loved one's thoughts and feelings. Impostors are interested in only one part of a person's life. For teen-agers this is often the other person's sexuality. Since this is the time for sexual excitement and discovery, it is easy for sexual attraction, which is good in itself, to be equated with love. The feelings and emotions of being sexually attracted to another are so new, so intense, so exciting that a young person may assume it is love.

2. Mature love *desires the highest good for the person loved.* Impostors are usually interested in self-gratification which is a natural experience during the puppy love stage, but it is inappropriate as a major factor in mature love. Mature love wants to make the other person happy and fulfilled, while the impostors want the other person to make them happy and meet their own needs. The deceivers do not worry about

hurting the other, causing heartache, sadness, and guilt, but mature love does not hurt. Sexually speaking, of course, this self-gratification is most prevalent when one partner wants the satisfaction of some kind of sexual expression that the other does not want to give. The male who says, "If you really love me, you would go to bed with me." is an example of self-gratification rather than kindness and concern for the feelings of the other. Love "does not rejoice at wrong, but rejoices in the right" (1 Cor. 13:6).

3. Real love is *trustworthy and trusting.* It is trustworthy because it is always honest with the other person. It does not depend on lying, cheating, or deceiving the other. It is trusting because it believes the other is being truthful and open. Impostors do not mind deceiving, being dishonest, or cheating the other person. Real love wears no mask, but the impostors do. Love "believes all things, hopes all things" (1 Cor. 13:7).

4. Real love is *consistent;* impostors are transient. Love can stand the tests of time and separation. Other feelings which seem to be love usually fade away after a time. One way a teen-ager can evaluate a relationship is simply to give it time. If time feeds the relationship and sustains it, then perhaps it is love. If it is infatuation, it will probably pass away Since everything in our world is in a hurry and there is always the press for time, it is difficult for many young people to use this criterion, but it is still a good one. "Love never ends" (1 Cor. 13:8).

5. Also it is true that love *grows* and *develops* rather than remaining stagnant. A true love relationship gets deeper, expands, finds out new things about the other person, and is continuously excited about new discoveries, new understandings, new communications. One can feel the strengthening of ties and the growing oneness of being together. The impostors usually become dull and stagnant. The same old words, the same old activities, the same old routines

make the relationship get boring. The concept of going steady makes it difficult to break these static relationships and both parties tend to argue, fight, or look for way-out thrills in order to overcome the boredom. As the impostors move along they don't explore the other person's mind or show new interests. The joy and excitement goes out of the relationship. (See Phil. 1:9.)

6. Mature love is not *blind*. It knows about the beloved person's weaknesses and shortcomings as well as their strengths and abilities. Real love accepts *all* of the other person, it does not expect to change the other to fit its image. Immature love is usually blind, unable to accept the realities about the other person. It refuses to see the weaknesses and shortcomings of the other. It pretends that the other is perfect, without fault, right in every thought and deed. This is nice for high school romance, but it rarely indicates a mature love. If you cannot love a person as he or she really is then your feelings are not mature love. We know that God sees us as we really are and loves us as we are. "Love bears all things, . . . endures all things" (1 Cor. 13:7).

7. Mature love is basically a *relationship of giving and receiving* rather than taking and demanding. Through the gift of his Son, God has demonstrated that love is giving. "For God so loved the world that he gave." So those who love give of themselves. They are not selfish. God also receives our love and is happy that we love him in return. "We love, because he first loved us" (1 John 4:19).

Immature love wants to take from the other, it demands satisfaction, and in extreme cases—slavery. When a relationship is draining on one party, when the meeting of needs goes only one way, when giving into demands is required by one party to keep the relationship alive, this is not real love. "Love is patient and kind" (1 Cor. 13:4).

8. Furthermore, mature love *grants freedom* to the other person; freedom to become independent, freedom to fulfil his or her own individuality, freedom to be one's self, freedom to explore life, freedom to meet some needs outside of the one loving relationship. Impostors are possessive. They seek control. They are jealous. They dampen the spirit and clamp down on individual expression. They cannot tolerate independence of thought or disagreement. "Love is not jealous or boastful; it is not arrogant or rude. Love does not insist on its own way; it is not irritable or resentful" (1 Cor. 13:4-5).

9. Mature love involves friendship. *Eros* is the Greek word describing love in its romantic, sexual, male-female expressions. *Philia* is the Greek word for love in its mutual friendship form. A mature loving relationship between male and female must involve both! When a young person feels in love with a person he or she does not *like,* that relationship is sexual attraction or some other emotion. It cannot be mature love!

The kind of mature love described in these paragraphs is the ideal which Christians should strive for in all their relationships, but it is extremely important when thinking of a heterosexual relationship which one hopes will develop into a meaningful, fulfilling, loving marriage.

Suggestions for Further Reading

Bailey, D. S. *Common Sense About Sexual Ethics: A Christian View.*

Pemberton, Prentiss L. *Dialogue in Romantic Love.* Valley Forge, Pennsylvania: The Judson Press, 1961.

Mazur, Ronald M. *Commonsense Sex.* Boston: Beacon Press, 1968.

Hulme, William. *Youth Considers Sex.* New York: Thomas Nelson & Sons, 1965.

Barnett, Len. *Sex and Teen-agers in Love.*

Steinke, Peter L. *Right, Wrong, or What?* St. Louis: Concordia Publishing House, 1970.

Witt, Elmer N. *Life Can Be Sexual.* St. Louis: Concordia Publishing House, 1967.

6. Sexual Intercourse Before Marriage?

Ron and Kate had reached a point where they needed to make some decision about sexual intercourse. They took time to discuss their mutual desires, personal motivations, future relationship, the emotional and biological risks, consequences that could develop, and their personal moral values. Many young people are caught in situations which are very romantic and sexually stimulating. Suddenly faced with the possibility of sexual intercourse, they find that they have no strong ideas about their *real* beliefs and feelings. The word *real* is used because many young people assume they have adopted a traditional Christian view (not to participate before marriage); but when faced with an actual situation, they really have little commitment to, nor understanding of, the traditional Christian stance.

You will handle your sexuality and make your decisions about sexual expression more maturely if you consider carefully the possible meanings of sexual intercourse in your life before getting into a situation where uncertainty can create a problem. You may have to update your thoughts and feelings every so often as your self-understanding, beliefs, and experiences change. Ultimately, you will make the final choice about whether to engage in premarital sexual intercourse. No one will decide for you. Hopefully, you will base your thinking and decision-making on knowledge of the potential hazards and measure this decision against basic Christian principles. In this chapter we will point out some of the things to be considered when making such decisions.

Immature Motivations

One factor needing evaluation is the motivation behind each partner's interest in sexual intercourse. It is possible to have mature motivations, but often the motivations behind the interest in sexual intercourse during teen-age years are immature.

Feelings of immaturity or childishness. Sometimes an individual young person, whether male or female, is plagued with feelings of immaturity or childishness. These feelings make them feel inferior and inexperienced alongside their friends and acquaintances. They may feel several years behind friends who seem to be sophisticated, "cool," wise, and "mature." These feelings are so strong and frustrating that the young person spends much emotional energy trying to find ways in which to overcome them.

Some young people decide that having sexual intercourse would prove their "adultness" or maturity. Like many other aspects of adolescent behavior, it is often assumed that a person who has achieved sexual intercourse is somehow more mature than the one who has not. It is possible that achieving sexual intercourse might make a young person feel more important, more accomplished, more "with it"—like making the football team or being elected to some office. However, negative factors which might be involved may make the possible gains insignificant.

As we have indicated in earlier sections of the book, sexual maturity is not related to the simple physical maneuver of sexual intercourse. Sexual maturity involves the establishment of meaningful heterosexual relationships. The young person who feels immature and childish needs to spend time developing such relationships, learning how to express real love through caring, being concerned, taking care of, sharing thoughts and feelings, and other mature expressions of real love.

Feelings of inadequacy. Some young people are burdened with a feeling of inferiority or inadequacy about their sexual identity. They doubt whether or not they can be attractive to members of the opposite sex. They are unsure whether or not they have anything to offer physically, emotionally, or mentally in a sexual relationship. They may worry that they are too much like the other sex—the girl worrying that she is too masculine and the boy worrying that he is too feminine.

Usually a person with these feelings withdraws from heterosexual contacts (which does not help), but others choose to overcompensate and try desperately to establish their masculinity or femininity through sexual conquests or seductions. The boy who "notches his gun" everytime he "scores," passes himself off as a great lover, relates to a date only in sexual ways and views her as a potential conquest—he is usually having difficulty accepting and feeling comfortable with his sexuality. He compensates by thinking that manliness and male maturity can be located in the genitals and that sexual intercourse proves he has these qualities.

The female who promiscuously plays "musical beds" with a number of men to win acceptance as a "sexy" girl, or the girl who must "lay" every day in order to demonstrate her femaleness, is usually having difficulty with her sexuality and is emotionally doubtful about her femininity.

As is obvious from the fact that continued sexual intercourse is not fulfilling or helpful to these persons, promiscuity and indiscriminate sexual intercourse is not the answer to establishing a healthy, mature, loving relationship.

Hostility. Another immature motivation, but one that is hard to discover, is the motivation of hostility. Hostility? Yes. As you have heard before, love and anger can be closely related. Sex can be an expression of either love or anger. For example, some young people choose to express their hostility toward authoritarian, dominating, or uncaring parents by engaging in sexual intercourse. Their purpose is to do something which will hurt the parent and thereby gain some measure of revenge. This is probably more common among girls, since they do not have as many avenues of rebellion against parents as do boys. Because of the double standard the girl is the one who is expected "to stay pure" and maintain her virginity. She knows that the same personal rigidity which causes parents to be authoritarian and domineering also makes them vulnerable to hurt when their children "let them down" or "disgrace" the family.

Because of the emphasis on "conquest" in our American patterns of courtship, aggression is sometimes the major motivation in dating behavior. When sexual intercourse is the goal of a lovemaking session, then conquest rather than love might be the unconscious goal. The vocabulary used by males to describe their sexual goals and fantasies are sometimes angry words like "make," "knock-up," and "score." Some young people enter into lovemaking like it was a contest in which they had to be the winner. Feelings of aggression which are expressed in sexual intercourse are usually destructive. Love is not the primary motivation and the sexual expression is in conflict with the Christian ethic.

The need for security and dependency. One other motivation should be mentioned. It is the need for security and dependency. Sometimes a girl's preoccupation with romantic ideas or her desire to marry so as not to be "an old maid" will motivate her to participate in, or initiate, sexual intercourse. "Participate in" refers to the girl who has decided against sexual intercourse before marriage, but when faced with either losing her boyfriend or agreeing to his demand for intercourse, she yields. A girl who takes the initiative may sense that her boyfriend is losing interest or beginning to have a "roving eye," and she decides to "give herself" to him in order to rekindle his feeling toward her and recapture his affection.

Recently I counseled with two boys who preferred ethically to hold sexual intercourse until marriage but said they were pushed into it to hold their girlfriends. The girlfriends told the boys that if they could not have sexual intercourse, they would look for other boyfriends. Neither boy could endure thinking that he was not "enough of a man" to satisfy his girlfriend sexually and gave in. So this need for security is present in both sexes.

The person who is motivated by a strong need for security or dependency is approaching sexual intercourse from an immature position. He needs to move toward establishing a personal independence and autonomy so he can make a more valid choice of sexual behavior. Most of all, "using" a partner for security or using sexual initiative as a way of manipulating a partner to stay in a relationship rejects the Christian ethic. Real love grants freedom to the loved person to choose his own lifestyle and to move in directions he or she chooses.

Future of the Relationship

Many young couples assume that sexual intercourse will increase and deepen their feelings toward each other. This is especially true of girls. Since this assumption is a major consideration, we must examine some of the effects which premarital sexual intercourse may have on the relationship.

Loss of respect. Since there is still a cultural bias against

premarital sexual intercourse, most young people have grown up with the idea in mind (even though it might not be conscious) that "good people" (particularly girls) should save sexual intercourse for marriage. Sometimes after a couple has had sexual intercourse, one or both partners lose respect for the other. Each may feel that the other one lowered his or her ethical standards. This loss of respect may turn into hostility if one partner lets other people know that sexual intercourse has taken place.

What would you really think of a person (even one you loved a great deal) who had premarital sexual intercourse? Would it make any difference in the way you felt about him or her? How would your feelings of respect change if you knew he or she had or would have sexual intercourse with someone beside yourself? These are questions which young people need to ask before committing themselves to this expression of love.

Committed or trapped? Sometimes a couple who experience sexual intercourse feel that this act has committed them to marriage. As a teen-ager you have many experiences yet to come (college, military service, joining the work force, traveling), and your freedom is important. If a feeling of making such a life-long commitment follows sexual intercourse, it may create resentment and a feeling of being cornered or trapped.

This increased feeling of commitment may also create jealous reactions when either partner relates to other males or females. One partner may hold on to a relationship longer than other factors indicate after sexual intercourse. Some couples get married because they have engaged in sexual intercourse when they might not have married otherwise.

How committed would you feel if you had sexual intercourse with your boyfriend or girlfriend? How much commitment would you expect from him or her? Do you really want to make that strong a commitment at the present time?

Is that all there is? It is no secret that the first experience of sexual intercourse, even for people who wait for the honeymoon, is usually not as romantic as anticipated. Teen-age experiences of sexual intercourse can be sabotaged by fear of discovery, guilt, uncertainty about procedures, feelings of awkwardness, embarrassment, and poor surroundings. When a sexual debut is spoiled, it can create feelings of disappointment and tension between the couple. Both may feel cheated, inadequate, or hostile toward the other for involving themselves in something that was negative.

This resulting disappointment or hostility may interrupt or terminate a relationship that could have otherwise developed into something mature and lasting. Can you be sure that the experience of sexual intercourse at this time would be a good experience and bring closeness or is it possible that it could spoil a good and growing relationship?

False sense of intimacy. The need for love, security, and intimacy is a strong one. The search for intimacy—mutual understanding and acceptance—is a major goal of young adults. You may be already feeling this need. Sexual intercourse is sometimes mistakenly equated with intimacy. Intercourse can be a significant aspect of intimacy and can be a vital communication of intimacy for those who are developing a mature love relationship.

Sexual intercourse itself, however, cannot bring this true intimacy! If you and your boyfriend or girlfriend are having a relationship which is stormy and superficial, you may decide that sexual intercourse could change that. Think twice, for intimacy which cannot be obtained without sexual intercourse will not be obtained through it.

Intimacy is a part of love and grows over a period of time. It involves knowing your partner at the deepest, most profound levels. Sexual intercourse can be an avenue to this "knowing."

You must also realize that sexual intercourse without this profound relationship does not usually reveal intimacy and in fact may stand in the way. Some young couples get so involved in sexual intimacies that the physiological preoccupation prevents the development of a relationship that is strong enough and deep enough to support a marriage relationship.

Future marriage. Some couples who have premarital sexual intercourse while dating or while engaged find later that the experience of sexual intercourse is something they cannot forget. Occasionally one partner becomes suspicious of the spouse. They ask such questions as, "If he would go to bed with me before our marriage, what would prevent him from going to bed with someone else after our marriage?" This kind of suspicion can be devastating to a marriage.

Personal Factors to Consider

A young person considering sexual intercourse must be aware of the effects which premarital sexual intercourse can have on his or her personal future. Some possibilities are:

Loss of self-esteem. How will sexual intercourse prior to marriage affect your feelings about yourself? If you have included virginity as an ideal in your self-concept, then to engage in coitus prior to marriage may be seen as a failure. If you have strong negative feelings toward sexuality, you might even feel dirty or contemptuous about yourself.

How would you feel about yourself if you experienced premarital sexual intercourse? Would you think lower of yourself? Or higher of yourself? Would you feel as good about yourself when you married?

Guilt. For the same reasons, you should consider the possibilities of feeling guilty about having premarital sexual intercourse. The Christian community has taught for centuries that premarital sexual intercourse is immoral. This teaching is based on a strong religious commitment and the valid feeling that premarital sexual intercourse can have many destructive consequences. To completely forget those teachings is very difficult. Only the most liberated and free individual can keep from having guilt feelings when acting contrary to the teachings, particularly the moral instruction, of his home and church. Do not underestimate the potential strength of feelings of guilt that may arise.

Future marriage. If you marry someone else, will you tell them about your previous experience? How would they react? What if you choose not to tell them and they find out later from somebody else? Ideally, a mature man or woman should be able to accept his partner's sexual past, forgive and forget (if necessary), just as with any other possible negative factor in a partner's life. In reality, however, many partners are not able to accept the fact that their spouse experienced sexual intercourse with another person. Males particularly are still caught up in the idea of sexual possessiveness. Although they may have been sexually promiscuous themselves, they often expect their wives to be totally "theirs." They expect to be "first" and cannot accept the fact that another man has had that privilege.

Sexual Compatibility

Bill is eighteen years old and will soon graduate from high school. Susan is sixteen and has one year left. After going steady three months they have talked vaguely about getting married after Bill graduates and gets a job. Bill had approached Susan about having intercourse with him by saying that he wanted to know before they got married whether they were sexually compatible and could make good "sex partners." He claimed his own parents had problems because they were not sexually compatible and that his older brother had separated from his wife because she was "as cold as a refrigerator."

Susan came to the counselor with this question, "Is finding out about sexual compatibility something we should do before marriage?" Susan's question is a good one and many young people have asked it. No marriage can reach its highest potential for joy, oneness, and love without sexual compatibility. While not the only component of a happy marriage, it is a major one. To downgrade the importance of sexual compatibility would be as big a mistake as overemphasizing it.

What is sexual compatibility? It is the ability and willingness of two persons to give and receive mutual pleasure, excitement, and joy from a full range of sexual expression, including intercourse. Full sexual compatibility transcends simple physcial pleasure and can exist only within a loving relationship which meets the prerequisites of mature love. Trust must be complete. The man must be made to feel adequate and masculine by the woman, and the woman must be made to feel secure, loved, and sexually attractive by the man.

As can be seen from this definition and description, sexual compatibility is basically a question of relationship not of "physical fitting." Sexual compatibility does not mean hooking up your sexual plumbing to see it it fits! Any physically normal male and physically normal female (which includes 99 percent of the population) can "fit together" sexually. Bill could go to a prostitute and have physically satisfying sexual intercourse. But that would not mean they were sexually compatible. It would only mean they were biologically capable of coitus. Sexual intercourse is basic to sexual compatibility, but by itself is not an indicator of whether a couple can be sexually happy.

Premarital sexual intercourse can actually give false indications about sexual compatibility. A couple might decide on experiencing intercourse with the result that, because of all the possible problems (fear of pain, fear of discovery, guilt, anxiety, doubt, premature ejaculation, etc.) , the experience might be very poor, even disgusting. Either one or both of the partners might be "turned off" by the experience and decide they are not suited partners.

Another couple might plan carefully, talk out their fears and guilts, experience intercourse under favorable physical conditions, and decide they were sexually compatible. Then they might use this experience as *the* major reason for getting married while overlooking the significant other factors that are part of sexual compatibility within marriage itself.

How can you evaluate sexual compatibility between you and the person you consider marrying? The most important and reliable gauge is the quality of your love. If love is mature and meets the criteria discussed in chapter 5, then it should include the ingredients necessary for sexual compatibility. Sex would be a means of giving and receiving love which already exists, rather than an attempt to establish something that is not present in the relationship.

Some girls and some boys are concerned about the sexual potential of their future mates. A boy may wonder if his steady could possibly turn out to be a "cold" or emotionally frigid woman. A girl could be concerned whether her sexual feelings are strong enough to be normal or whether she might be unresponsive. "Frigidity" is a concept widely communicated in popular literature for both males and females. There are adequate signs within a loving relationship, however, to indicate whether a person will be sexually responsive.

One aspect of your loving relationship will be the imagination and fantasy which you will have about your partner. If you can imagine yourself physically and emotionally sharing sexuality with your partner, it is good evidence that you will be able to respond sexually after marriage. Because most people have a desire for sexual intercourse, this desire itself gives clues to sexual responsiveness.

The actual lovemaking that takes place in your relationship should give further clues. If the girl can respond to the lovemaking with the man she is in love with and feel the warm, tender, surrendering feelings that are part of sexuality, then it would be difficult to imagine her as a frigid person. Many couples will experience enough intensity in their lovemaking, such as Ron and Kate, that they will have no doubts about the sexual interest and potential for full sexual relationship that exists in each of them.

Sometimes the male who disagrees with the ethical limits set by his female partner may mistakenly interpret these limits as "coldness." If your girlfriend enjoys being a woman, can talk about sexuality, enjoys the degree of lovemaking which she allows, and is free with her emotions and feelings, then you need not worry about her sexual interest. The girl should be able to ask herself these same questions. If the answer to these concerns is yes, then she can be assured of her emotional and physical sexual potential.

If you have fears about sexual experience or have undergone some sexual trauma which has created negative feelings about sexuality, then you might want to talk with some professional person who could help you evaluate your sexual growth and development and your potential for sexual responsiveness.

Suggestions for Further Reading

Duvall, Evelyn M. *Why Wait Till Marriage?* New York: Association Press, 1965.

Kirkendall, Lester A. *Premarital Intercourse and Interpersonal Relationships.* New York: The Julian Press, 1961.

Fromm, Erich. *The Art of Loving.* New York: Bantam Books, 1963.

Barnett. *Sex and Teen-agers in Love.* (See chapter 4.)

Hulme. *Youth Considers Sex.* (See chapter 5.)

7. Unwanted Pregnancy, Birth Control, Venereal Disease

Unwanted Pregnancy

It would be appropriate to begin this chapter with an important but often overlooked fact: *any time sexual intercourse occurs* (assuming that both partners are fertile) *conception is a possibility!* You might be thinking, "Well, everyone knows that." Perhaps so, but since the number of unwanted pregnancies occurring outside of marriage steadily increases, one must conclude that many young people refuse to face this fact. Few couples want or expect a pregnancy before marriage.

Your next thought might be, "Well, why don't these young people use birth control?" A good question but one that brings up another overlooked truth. The italicized statement above is true *even when contraceptives are used!* Yes, it is true that birth control methods and the use of contraceptives (particularly the pill) can reduce to a minimum the statistical possibility of conception. You should remember, however, that at this time *no* form of contraception is 100 percent effective. Contraceptive devices may be applied improperly, they may break, they may not be available, and contraceptive chemicals may not work the same on every person. Many couples, both married and unmarried, have experienced a failure of contraceptives which has allowed pregnancy to occur despite the supposed protection.

Are you thinking how nice it will be when a 100 percent effective birth control method is discovered and becomes available? You are right. It will be very helpful. However, another problem will still exist: *many young people do not use contraceptives during their first experience of sexual intercourse.* Idealistic teen-agers often assume they will not participate in sexual intercourse prior to marriage, even though they may never have made any strong commitment to that decision nor have carefully thought out their position. Then they get carried away during an exciting experience of lovemaking without weighing the risk of pregnancy and without taking the time or making the effort to use contraceptives. Counselors, pastors, and parents hear over and over: "I never thought that could happen," or "We thought that this one time would probably be okay," or "We didn't plan on doing that." So it will be a long time before the subject of unwanted pregnancy can be left out of books on sex.

Unwanted pregnancies are not fun for anybody—there are *no* winners. In such circumstances the best one can hope for is that the degree of hurt, misunderstanding, and personal chagrin, will be minimal. Let's look at the parties involved.

The pregnant young woman (mother-to-be) usually bears the brunt of such an experience. She may experience the most disappointment—in herself and in the father. She may have to deal with the most guilt—for becoming pregnant out of wedlock, for causing her parents such distress, and for her part in the uncertain situation for the child. She is the one who is primarily responsible for making the painful decision about how to handle the pregnancy.

First, she may consider whether to terminate the pregnancy immediately through the process of therapeutic abortion. If she allows the pregnancy to go full term, she must decide whether to leave town to have the baby or risk public censure by staying at home. After bearing the child, she must decide whether to keep the baby or put it up for adoption. Any choice is less than ideal and may result in feelings of being unfair or unjust to the child. She must also decide whether or not to marry the father.

The father is still not treated as roughly by society nor talked about as much as the unwed mother. If he was involved sexually with the girl because of immature motives (such as exploitation or manipulation) and interested only superficially in the girl, he may not care what happens. More often, however, the father is involved with feelings of his own and experiences anxiety about the situation. If he loves and cares for the girl, he will probably regret his share of the responsibility for what she is going through. He also may have acted contrary to his ethical principles and experience strong feelings of guilt and loss of self-esteem. He must face the probable disappointment of both his parents and her parents.

If she took the sexual initiative, he may feel that the girl has trapped him into sexual activity which he did not want to pursue and resent the consequences. The father may be involved in the decisions about abortion and whether the woman keeps the baby or puts it up for adoption. He, too, participates in the decision about whether or not to marry.

The father may make the mistake of pretending he loves the girl enough to marry her in order to relieve a guilty conscience or to fulfil a commitment he has not really made emotionally. This may result in a premature marriage based more on the accidental pregnancy than on maturing love.

The family and friends of the two people involved may by disappointed, embarrassed, and hurt by what they may feel to be an immoral act. If these people are significant people in the lives of the father and mother and have strong negative feelings toward sexual experience before marriage, they can create a very negative atmosphere, which makes the mother-to-be and

the father-to-be feel inferior and guilty. Some parents are able to handle the stiuation with maturity and help with the problem instead of being part of it.

If the pregnancy is allowed to continue and birth occurs, some thought should be given to the child. Because of the number of families wanting to adopt children and because of the care of adoption agencies in seeking good homes, the infant given up for adoption will in all probability be raised in an excellent home where he will be cared for, provided for, and loved very much.

If the child is kept by the mother, other things must be considered. If she is forced to keep the child because of family or religious pressure, resentment may cause her either to mistreat, neglect, and abuse the child; or she may try to hide her resentment by being overprotective and "smothering" in her care of the child. Each has a serious effect on the child's personal growth and development. The child may be resented as a liability in the future when the girl desires to live the life of a single person, date, and marry.

If you should become pregnant, or if you should impregnate your girlfriend, seek some professional counseling. A doctor, counselor, pastor, or psychiatrist can help you sort out all of these possibilities, deal honestly with your feelings, and help you handle this dilemma responsibly.

Birth Control

Birth control information for teen-agers is an emotionally charged subject. Opinions run the gamut from those who think contraceptives should be given to all teen-agers to those who think any unmarried person using contraceptives is a sinner.

Those who suggest distribution of information and contraceptive devices to teen-agers feel that unwanted pregnancies should be avoided at any cost. They realistically realize that many teen-agers engage in premarital sexual intercourse resulting in many unwanted pregnancies. They are also aware that when many teen-agers do engage in sexual intercourse it is usually spontaneous and unplanned. It is not true that all people in favor of making birth control information and devices available to teen-agers are immoral people who believe in "free sex" and sexual promiscuity.

Those who oppose the idea of giving any birth control information to teens usually feel that such action will open the floodgates of permissiveness. They are afraid that teen-agers will be more likely to engage in sexual behavior, even sexual orgies, if such information and devices are made available to them. They do not have a positive view of the adolescent's ability and potential for handling sexual drives and desires in a responsible manner. They have a realistic concern that the immature teen-ager will use contraceptives as a ticket to promiscuity. The extremists label efforts at planned parenthood and information about birth control as a Communist plot. It is also a sad fact that some adults are against making birth control information available because they think a girl who is "loose" should suffer the consequences (pregnancy) and be forced to bear the child.

The most appropriate and ethically valid approach is one which makes information on birth control available to all teen-agers and provides conception control devices for those who request them. Three established facts support this position:

1. The number of pregnancies outside of marriage has continued to increase significantly in recent years with the following negative results: (a) more unwanted children, (b) more abortions, and (c) more unwise and premature marriages. The number of times these negative results occur could be significantly reduced if young people had the knowledge and freedom which would allow them to be more responsible with

their sexual potential.

2. The number of young people engaging in premarital sexual intercourse is increasing. The present increase is probably not as extreme as many people fear, but it is still true that more young people are having sexual intercourse before marriage. In a study by the President's Commission on Population Growth and the American Future, released in May, 1972, for example, 46 percent of the unmarried females interviewed had experienced sexual intercourse by age nineteen. Obviously the percentage of males having such experience would be even higher. This means of course that the potential for pregnancy continues to increase.

3. Knowledge of contraception *can* enhance a teen-ager's feelings of responsibility rather than loosening his moral values. No studies have indicated that sexual promiscuity increases with knowledge of sexuality and specific knowledge of birth control. On the other hand, misinformation does contribute to the number of unwanted pregnancies. The same study mentioned above indicated that many teen-age girls are misinformed about the time during their menstrual cycle when they are most likely to become pregnant. It also indicated that the failure to use contraceptives contributed to the high pregnancy risks of teen-agers.

Moral-ethical concerns about birth control. What moral-ethical considerations should be discussed about this subject? We are not talking now about the pros and cons of sexual intercourse prior to marriage. This has been discussed in previous chapters. Now we are looking at the question of the morality of conception control for those who decide to participate in sexual intercourse as a part of their lovemaking. When two people—married or single—engage in sexual intercourse, they must realize that the potential for conception is present. They can choose to allow that potential to remain or they can reduce it significantly by choosing to use a contraceptive. One reason it is so important for Christian young people to decide about sexual intercourse is the responsibility they have for making ethical decisions about controlling conception.

The male sperm and the female ovum are wonderful parts of human sexuality, having the potential to unite and eventually form a new human being. Since this procreative potential is a sacred trust, it must be taken seriously. We have already discussed the problems existing in having an unwanted pregnancy. Responsible parenthood is something to be considered at all times, not just after marriage. This should be the primary ethical consideration at this point.

Giving birth to children demands the willingness and the resources to parent a child, to love it, to protect it, to give it nurture, and provide a rich environment which will foster growth and development into mature adulthood. Few teenagers are ready emotionally or financially to take on such a responsibility. Most young people would not desire pregnancy prior to marriage if given a choice. Therefore, the teen-ager who participates in sexual intercourse, or who allows the lovemaking in which he or she becomes involved to lead in that direction, should be willing to take ethical responsibility for the conception possibilities inherent in sexual intercourse. Using some contraceptive method to avoid unwanted pregnancy is more ethical than chancing the conception of an unwanted child.

If you are a young woman, your body will produce about four hundred eggs in your lifetime. Each egg has the potential to be fertilized by a male sperm and develop into a child. Someday you will probably want to parent a child. At that time, conception, pregnancy, and birth are aspects of a very special event which will mean much to you and your husband. *You* have responsibility for *if* and *when* these eggs are fertilized. You are responsible for deciding if and when you want to give birth to and mother a child. Not to think about this trust is to be less than mature, less than responsible.

If you are a young man, your body will produce millions of sperm in your lifetime. Each has the capability of fertilizing a woman's egg resulting in conception. *You* have as much responsibility under God as does the woman for this act of procreation. Parenting is something in which both father and mother should be involved. For you to treat your sexual potential irresponsibly is unethical.

When either partner apathetically leaves contraception up to the other, then each is being irresponsible. Both should be concerned and mutually accept responsibility for preventing an unwanted pregnancy. Hopefully, you will take this responsibility all your lives so that parenting will be by choice and not by accident. Remember—your potentiality for procreation is a sacred trust.

For those who have decided on engaging in sexual intercourse prior to marriage there is also the ethical consideration demanded by a loving relationship. Does a young man want to put a girl in the position of having to consider an abortion, giving a child up for adoption, raising a child by herself, or marrying when there is not an adequate reason? Does a girl want to take this risk? Does either partner want to be involved in the problems related to unwanted pregnancies? Certainly prevention of conception is the responsible option for those who choose to engage in sexual intercourse. That choice may be a conscious decision or it may come by just getting into emotionally and physically vulnerable situations (such as continued heavy lovemaking, with fondling of the genitals, little or no clothing, mutual orgasms, etc.) which often lead to sexual intercourse.

If you do not have a good knowledge of contraception, find out from some competent professional person. Check with planned parenthood organizations, a doctor you trust, a sex educator at school, or the YMCA and YWCA. Many books can give you explicit information about birth control techniques.

Venereal Disease

Those who engage in sexual intercourse must also consider the possibility of venereal infection. In recent years the incidence of venereal disease in the United States has increased alarmingly. The American Medical Association has warned that venereal disease has reached epidemic proportions.

What is venereal disease? "Venereal" comes from the old word "venery," meaning sexual intercourse. Venereal diseases, then, are those associated with sexual intercourse. The most common in our country are two bacterial infections called gonorrhea and syphilis.

How is venereal disease spread? A person is usually infected by a venereal disease only during sexual intercourse, or some other intimate genital contact, with a person who is already infected. In rare cases infection can come from oral or anal contact or from the symptomatic sores. It is highly improbable for these bacteria to spread from towels, toilet seats, etc., because they live on human bodies and cannot live outside the body.

Why worry about venereal disease? Although some young people tend to equate venereal disease with mild medical problems such as dandruff, athlete's foot, and "jock itch," venereal disease can, in fact, be very destructive. Venereal disease can cause sterility in both males and females, meaning you become non-fertile and cannot produce children. Pregnant women infected with venereal disease often miscarry or give birth to defective and diseased children. Syphilis, in its later stages, can cause damage to essential body systems which can result in death. The nervous system is often so diseased that serious mental and physical illness such as blindness, paralysis, and insanity result.

How can you recognize venereal disease? Symptoms of gonorrhea include: (1) pain in the penis or vagina, particularly a burning sensation when urinating, (2) a milky or watery discharge from the penis or the vagina, which is very infectious and can spread to the eyes and throat, (3) general soreness and swelling in the genital area, (4) the urge to urinate frequently. The main sympton of syphilis is the development of an open sore or lesion about the size of a fingernail in the genital area—usually the female labia or the male penis. This sore can also develop in the mouth or on the lips. The sore usually appears ten to fourteen days after infection actually occurs but may not appear until many weeks later. Secondary signs may include a rash on the skin and sores in the mouth, on the palms of the hands, or on the soles of the feet.

One characteristic of venereal disease is that the original symptoms (mentioned above) are not only hard to detect, but they may disappear. This disappearance seems to be a healing period. In fact, the infection just "goes underground." You are still infected! The bacteria is still potentially destructive within your body and can be given to others.

How can you avoid venereal disease? The only way to avoid venereal disease is to avoid sexual intimacies with those who are infected. Of course you cannot know for sure who is and who is not infected. It may be present in any group of people, including well-educated people, people who live in the suburbs, and church members. If you insist on taking this risk, you can minimize the chance of catching or spreading infection by using a condom ("rubber").

What can you do if infected? If you suspect that you are

infected with a venereal disease, or that you have been exposed to infection, you should see a doctor immediately! Many physicians will see you privately without having to talk with your parents—call and ask. Your local county health department can help you locate a doctor and may operate a VD clinic. Luckily, venereal disease can be cured quite simply in its early stages by proper medical attention, usually a program of treatment with antibiotics. But remember—venereal diseases do not cure themselves. They will continue to infect you, make you contagious, and threaten your health until you receive medical attention!

Venereal disease and the Christian ethic. Venereal diseases are popularly thought of as something immoral or evil rather than as a medical problem. This attitude exists because venereal disease is a disease originating from sexual intercourse, usually outside of marriage. Having venereal disease, then, becomes something like a mark of immorality. Some people even consider it God's punishment on people "who live by the flesh." Such a belief does not square with the New Testament concept of love, mercy, forgiveness, and acceptance. Having a venereal disease is not immoral in itself, even if you believe that sexual intercourse outside of marriage is immoral.

Whether or not your moral stance includes and accepts sexual intercourse before marriage, you have a moral obligation not to spread venereal disease. Since venereal disease is obviously harmful to persons, it is a breach of the principle of love to risk infecting other people. The ethical person must assume responsibility for being aware of the possibilities of contracting a venereal disease, checking to see if he has the infection, and taking medical precautions against spreading the bacteria to others. It would be unethical to allow venereal disease to go unchecked and risk gradual destruction of your own mental and physical health. Nor is it a loving choice to endanger the health of other partners (such as your future marriage partner) and of children which you might later bring into existence.

Suggestions for Further Reading

Mace, David R. *Abortion: The Agonizing Decision.* Nashville: Abingdon Press, 1972.
See books listed in chapters 5 and 6.

8. Pornography

What is Pornography?

Pornography could be broadly defined as "erotic materials which present sex in a disgusting, lewd, or obscene manner." It is difficult, however, to describe specific pornographic materials, for although many people would agree to this broad definition, they have different opinions on what is disgusting or obscene. Two people agreeing with this general definition might strongly disagree about whether a particular book or picture was pornographic. Ideas about what is pornographic change with time and generations. You may find a difference between your ideas of what is disgusting and the ideas of your parents or your church. This creates a difference of opinion about what you should see or read.

Some people would disagree entirely with the above definition. Some believe that nothing is pornographic and that portrayal of sex in any shape or form is appropriate and educational. Others believe that anything sexual, or portraying sexuality in any way, is pornography and therefore immoral and not to be read or seen. Since the Christian cannot believe that sexuality is evil, his definition of "disgusting, lewd, or obscene" must include the portrayals of sexuality which are contrary to Christian principles about this aspect of creation and God's will for its use. An appropriate definition of pornography, therefore, would be "literature or photography which portrays sex in its perverted, misused, emotionally sick dimensions." Included in this definition are those ideas of sex which promote masochism and sadism (sexual contact in which one party causes pain through whippings, beatings, or burnings, and the other partner enjoys being treated in this manner); those which make sex ugly, evil, and dirty; and those that proclaim conquest as a major goal of sexuality.

Much current literature, photography, and other art forms are purposefully designed to stimulate sexual curiosity and excitement within the reader or viewer. The sexual content is designed to represent some of the realistic life-situations of which sex is an integral part. These materials are not usually pornographic and can add to your understanding of human sexuality in both its positive and destructive manifestations. Since it is difficult to make a clear distinction between these materials and those materials which are pornographic, this discussion will include both types of material under the category of "sexual materials."

Teen-agers and Sexual Materials

You may have already seen and read numerous examples of sexual materials (including pornography). To be curious about sex and sexuality is neither abnormal nor immoral. To read and look at these materials is not unusual for teen-agers. It has not yet been proven that there is any relationship between the use of sexual materials and the incidence of destructive sexual behavior.

It is possible that you can learn many things by observing the calloused, manipulative, and impersonal ways in which sex and sexuality is experienced and practiced by various people in various types of relationships. Remember, however, that sexual materials do not always convey *correct* information about sex or about the sexual feelings of most human beings.

Exposure to sexual materials is not wrong any more than exposure to other aspects of the human predicament, such as war, political intrigue, racial prejudice, or environmental destruction. The mature teen-ager does not see virtue in running around protecting himself from exposure to sexuality. Instead he or she concentrates on developing a healthy Christian view of sexuality in order to discern what is good and what is bad, what is responsible and what is irresponsible, what is loving and what is despising, what is beautiful and what is ugly, and what builds up and what tears down.

Problems with Using Sexual Materials

Using sexually oriented materials can cause or contribute to a teen-ager's personal problems, particularly with sexual development. To evaluate adequately and accurately your use of sexual materials, you should be aware of the possible negative results.

One danger of constant exposure to sexual materials is the possibility of accepting *negative* views of sex and sexuality as truth. The particular view of sex often portrayed by these materials—that is the separation of sex from love, beauty, tenderness, and ethical values—may be adopted by the young person as a valid sexual philosophy. Some sexual materials do justice to the various positive meanings, values, and beauties of sexuality, but others make sexuality dirty and ugly. Be careful not to accept blindly the philosophies of sexuality which are "preached" through some of today's sexual materials.

A second negative result of using sexual materials is the repulsive and sickened feeling which readers or viewers may have toward sex and sexuality as a result of the philosophy or content of certain sexual materials. As has been said, sex is basically good and healthy. When a young person views sex and sexuality in its misused, disgusting, and impersonal forms, he or she may have a strong negative emotional reaction. This negative feeling may effect his or her willingness to pursue healthy sexual goals in real life.

The third problem with sexual materials is their tendency to promote sexual experience as an end or goal in itself, They leave out the fact that sex, to be truly healthy, must be integrated into the rest of life and related to personal relationships, other human needs, and most of all, love.

You may react to sexual materials in a strongly negative or inappropriate manner. If you evaluate your reactions in this light, then take some steps to understand why. A person who has been taught that his or her body is forbidden territory and the source of evil temptations might become extremely anxious when viewing photography which is· sexually oriented. Someone who has learned that any sexual lovemaking is wrong and evil might become very upset when exposed to materials in which lovemaking occurs, particularly if it is portrayed as illicit lovemaking.

Exposure to sexually oriented materials might be so repulsive that it makes you physically ill. It might give you such an emotional shock that you find yourself unable to think of sex positively anymore. You could become afraid of dating, disgusted with the opposite sex, and ashamed of your own body. If this happens, then the book or movie may have uncovered negative attitudes and feelings about sexuality which already may have developed in your personality. This kind of reaction needs to be checked out with a competent adult who can help you discover how experiences, thoughts, and feelings in your past have caused such intense negative reactions.

Young people often use erotic materials to stimulate themselves sexually. Males often keep a collection of photographs and posters featuring nude or semi-nude women available for this purpose. They also read magazines and novels which describe varieties of sexual situations. These photographic and literary materials are used to activate sexual feelings and provide a focus for fantasy about one's own sexual desires. Females also read romantic-erotic magazines and books to provide themselves with sexual excitement. They often daydream about these stories and pretend they themselves are living the lives of the people portrayed in this literature.

Using sexual materials in these ways is not abnormal during the adolescent period of development. However, if your fantasies about sexual relationships include unhealthy and destructive ways of lovemaking or relating to the opposite sex (such as causing physical pain or emotional hurt to the partner or enjoying hurt and pain given by the partner during sexual experience), then something is short-circuiting your sexual growth and development. The same would be true if you find yourself constantly using sexual materials about homosexuality and fantasizing about participation in this type of lovemaking. You should ask some professional to help you explore the causes of these thoughts and attitudes.

Becoming overly dependent on sexual materials is another negative possibility to guard against. It is natural for an adolescent to experience sexual satisfaction from provocative materials. If sexual photography and literature are used constantly for sexual stimulation, however, then heterosexual development could be jeopardized. As a teen-ager you should be spending time and energy in getting acquainted and developing friendships with people of the opposite sex. This should be happening in real life, not just in your fantasies. If you are more interested in the "paper people" found in sexual literature and photography than the "real people" in your own environment (church, school, clubs), then something is wrong.

Evaluate whether your dependency on sexual literature and photography for sexual outlet and stimulation is healthy or unhealthy. If you are in doubt, have some competent person help you make that decision.

One way to check out the values or anti-values in the literature you read and the photography you see is to have some trusted adult friend with whom you can talk over your feelings and responses to what you see and read. He or she can help you measure the content and the meanings against the Christian values talked about earlier in this book. Ask your church for a course on "Christianity and Sexuality" for both adults and teen-agers taught by competent professional people. Request that the church provide you with accurate and realistic sexual literature through its library.

9. Homosexuality

In this book the term "homosexuality" refers to the sexual identity of those individuals who "constantly receive sexual gratification from persons of the same sex and prefer this type of sexual stimulation rather than relationships with those of the opposite sex." This chapter is included because most people your age must come to terms with homosexuality in both themselves and in other people.

Society and the Homosexual

Despite the fact that homosexuality is more openly discussed and publicized in this generation, most people in our culture have strong negative feelings about homosexuals and homosexuality. Homosexuals, particularly males, are ridiculed and stigmatized. They are occasionally treated cruelly, physically beaten, blackmailed, threatened, run out of town, and some of their civil rights are limited by law. They are described by some as mentally sick and portrayed as a menace to children. These prevailing feelings and attitudes are based on misconceptions.

In many ways, most homosexuals are not different from other people. They are not basically evil. They are not usually mentally ill, although like other people they do suffer from emotional problems. Homosexuality is not a mental illness but a sexual immaturity. A homosexual is someone who has not fully developed the psychosexual aspect of his or her personality. Many homosexuals contribute to the common good, and some famous people, were homosexuals, like Michelangelo and Walt Whitman.

Christianity and Homosexuality

Part of our society's negative feeling toward homosexuality grows out of the Christian tradition. The destruction of Sodom and Gomorrah told in Genesis 19 (and the origin of our word "sodomy" to refer to "unnatural" sexual acts) has been interpreted by both Christians and Jews through the centuries to mean that God's wrath would be visited on homosexuals. It is hard to imagine, however, the God of love rejecting human beings because of the psychological condition of homosexuality anymore than he would reject an individual suffering from emotional illness or mental retardation. Just because homosexual people fall short of their human potential does not mean they are outside of God's mercy and acceptance.

Homosexuality is not ideal. Like divorce, war, and many other things in life, it falls short of God's will for man. God, however, is always faithful to understand and love his creation despite its weakness and failures.

The Problem of Homosexuality

It is important to overcome irrational negative feelings and attitudes toward the homosexual. It is also important to consider realistically and understand the difficulties, problems, and disillusionments which plague the homosexual.

The way in which society treats homosexuals creates problems for them. The feelings of rejection, fear, and low self-esteem are emotions that have to be faced. They must face the designation of "abnormal" put upon them by society. If married, as many homosexuals are, they must worry about what will happen to their family if they are found out. They must wonder about what their spouses and children feel if they know or find out about the sexual problem.

The homosexual often leads an unfulfilled life because he or she cannot experience the heights of sexual completeness and oneness in intimate heterosexual relationships. By the nature of creation it is impossible for two people of the same sex to experience genital intercourse. The incompleteness of their sexual identity and the inability to fulfil sexual potential, often leaves the homosexual frustrated, lonely and dissatisfied.

At the core of sexuality, as created by God, is the mutual complementarity of male and female. The Christian belief about creation suggests that only a member of the opposite sex can really fulfil the sexual incompleteness of any individual. The truth is suggested in Genesis 2, where man's need for intimate relationships is not met with some representative of the animal world, but with someone like himself, yet different enough so that they could fulfil and complement one another.

The need for love and intimacy is basic to human existence. Basic to the deepest, most profound intimacy of which man is capable is sexual intercourse (genital) and the complementarity of the male-female differences. The homosexual, by virtue of his or her physiology and his or her confused sexual identity, cannot obtain this deeper level of intimacy.

Causes of Homosexuality

Exactly what causes homosexuality is not yet known, but many possibilities exit. Some studies have suggested that heredity might be a factor. This is particularly true with reference to the functioning of certain glands in the body and the balance of hormones. Other authorities dismiss this as an insignificant factor. Some authorities think that the pattern for homosexuality is established during childhood when the child overidentifies and gets too close to the parent of the opposite sex.

Certainly one significant factor in homosexuality is the failure of a person to move effectively into heterosexual patterns of behavior during puberty and adolescence. A young person may feel that he or she is not physically attractive, or that his or her personality is one that is unlikeable or inadequate. Early experiences or attempts at heterosexuality may be awkward or create anxiety. The young person may feel rejected by members of the opposite sex. Any of these feelings may cause the person to withdraw from contact with the opposite sex. Since the sex drive is usually expressed in some way toward another human person, the only choice left is someone of the same sex.

Another reason for homosexuality is a development of hostility toward, or fear of, the opposite sex. Harriet had lived with an alcoholic father who beat her constantly, was extremely strict and demanding, and never demonstrated any love. When she was eight years of age, a middle-aged male neighbor tried to have sexual intercourse with her. This traumatic event and the fear and hostility she felt toward her father affected her feelings toward all men. She was never able to relax or be interested in relating romantically to males. She was suspicious of them and fearful of them. Now she is seventeen and her sexual interest is directed toward a young female physical education instructor who has invited Harriet over to her house and made sexual overtures. Harriet gets no special charge from the sexual contact; in fact it makes her feel a little unsure, but the warm personal relationship is extremely important since she does not allow herself to experience any intimate feelings with males.

Another cause of homosexuality is brought on by an

overidentification during puberty. During the homosexual phase of sexual development it is normal for both sexes to form groups and gangs which are very meaningful to one another and with whom they spend a great deal of time. Those children who do not get into one of the groups during this period of life, from say eight to thirteen, will feel left out and isolated. One way of handling this feeling of isolation is to copy and idolize the people who are in the gang. The person continues to admire those of his or her own sex and to idolize the qualities and characteristics which they wish they had. Healthy self-esteem, therefore, is one major protection against homosexuality.

Your Experiences with Homosexuality

Studies show that about one out of three men engage in some kind of homosexual act in his lifetime, usually during childhood or adolescence. Many others have been sexually aroused by other males and many others have been approached by homosexuals. About one out of six females participates in a homosexual encounter in her life time. You can see that it would not be unusual for many readers to have had some type of homosexual contact or experience.

It is important to draw a clear distinction between *having* homosexual experience and *being* a homosexual! We have already defined homosexuality as a preference for sexual gratification from members of the same sex. A homosexual experience is one in which two people of the same sex indulge in some type of sexual stimulation. Participating in a homosexual experience does not mean that an individual is a permanent homosexual!

You may have had homosexual contact with friends during early adolescence when curiosity about sex motivated you to find out more about it. Examining the genitals of a friend or engaging in masturbation with a groups of friends is not unusual. Comparison of penis size and erection abilities has happened between numerous adolescent males. Girlfriends sometimes feel each other's breasts and occasionally manipulate each other's genitals in order to bring about orgasm.

As a result of these experiences you may feel that you are homosexual. One fifteen-year-old, boy worried because he had talked one of his younger neighbors into masturbating him about three years earlier. Tom thought this meant he had a homosexual personality. Another boy, Fred, had several homosexual experiences of genital manipulation with an uncle during camping trips and thought this indicated he was homosexual. Neither boy was actually a homosexual person.

Other young people worry because of their physical appearance. Some people believe they can spot a homosexual because of physical characteristics. Some young people accept this as true. They feel that if a male is effeminate, artistic, or has a high pitched voice he must be homosexual. Or if a woman is muscular, strong, or interested in sports she must be a lesbian. In fact, physical characteristics are *not* related to homosexuality! Many female homosexuals are very feminine and attractive. Many male homosexuals are muscular and athletic. Most experts think that homosexuality is a result of complex psychological and social factors with biological makeup only a minor aspect of the problem.

Let it be said again: having engaged in some kind of homosexual activity, either with a friend or with an older person, does not necessarily mean that you are homosexual! How can you know whether your tendencies toward homosexuality are stronger than they should be? You should be concerned about your sexual identity if you (1) center your strongest affections on friends of the same sex and never feel any affection toward members of the opposite sex, (2) if you frequently desire to view the nude bodies, either in photographs or in person, of members of your own sex, (3) if you fantasize or daydream continuously about homosexual relationships, or (4) if you desire frequent physical contact and anticipate playing with the genitals of members of the same sex. If any of these statements describe your feelings, then you need to consider that there *are* some problems in your sexual development and seek some professional help.

It is popularly thought that a person with homosexual feelings cannot be helped. This is not true! Many adolescents who are inclined toward homosexual relationships or who are actually involved in homosexuality can be helped toward heterosexuality. Of course this can best be accomplished by a professional, such as a psychiatrist, clinical psychologist, doctor, or counselor. Get a trusted adult to introduce you to someone who can help.

If you definitely do not consider yourself strongly leaning toward homosexuality you may still be concerned that your sexual feelings and thoughts are not growing and developing toward heterosexuality. You can also get some outside assistance. You need to put more energy into accepting yourself, particularly your sexuality. You need to take more initiative in getting involved with members of the opposite sex. This will give you the experience with them that you need to free you up for heterosexual relationships.

10. A Final Word

It is impossible for me to know what you as one young person think and feel about sex. Nor do I know what you have experienced sexually. You may be concerned about your lack of experience. Maybe you have not had much opportunity to date, have little interest in the opposite sex, still do not feel free around them, or for some other reason you have had little involvement with lovemaking and other sexual experiences.

Having limited sexual experience is usually no reason to feel left out. Everyone has his or her own timetable for sexual development that is affected by many things, including physical heredity (rate of maturity, glandular function) and environment (interests, social involvement, family background). Trust your experience, it is a valuable indicator of your readiness for sexual involvement.

Or you may have focused much attention on sex and sexuality so far in your life and have been involved in all types of sexual experiences. You may have experimented with many types of sexual expression and even participated in sexual intercourse. If these experiences have been negative, destructive, or irresponsible, I hope you will not dismiss sex as disillusioning, bad, or unnecessary, nor "write off" the opposite sex. Hopefully this book has offered ideas which will help you re-evaluate your sexual identity, examine the criteria

with which you have made decisions about sexual expression, and attain a good and healthy attitude toward this gift. Remember the love, forgiveness, and mercy of God, and know that he is intensely interested in helping you establish a mature sexual identity and experience meaningful heterosexual relationships.

Whatever your level of sexual experience, this book has attempted to help you examine this experience in order to evaluate the growth and development of your sexual identity, the maturity with which you think and feel about sexuality, and the ethical principles upon which you base your sexual expression. It is hoped that you will discover where you are at this point in your sexual development and maturely plan your future as a sexual being. Note that neither the lack of sexual experience nor the abundance of sexual adventure is necessarily related to sexual maturity. Many young people with little experience through high school are developing healthy and maturing sexual identities. Other young people who have had extensive sexual experience are still confused and uncertain about mature sexuality.

I hope that this book has clearly communicated that the Christian faith has good news for man about the purpose and meaning of sexuality! Christians can offer the world an understanding of the potential for fulfilment, satisfaction, and love which exists in the sexual aspects of personal relationships between men and women. The Christian gospel includes the proclamation—"Thank God for sex!" Sex is an important part of God's creation and an integral part of our lives. If we are to live the "abundant life" Jesus has promised us, we must successfully integrate sex into our personhoods. May God be with you.